İlham Dilman is Reader in Philosophy at the University College of Swansea. He is the author of *Sense and Delusion* (with D.Z. Phillips) (1971), *Induction and Deduction* (1973), *Matter and Mind* (1975), *Morality and the Inner Life* (1979), *Studies in Language and Reason* (1981), and *Freud and Human Nature* (1983).

D0984074

Freud and the Mind

To John Wisdom

Freud and the Mind

İlham Dilman

Basil Blackwell

© İlham Dilman 1984

First published 1984
Basil Blackwell Publisher Limited
108 Cowley Road, Oxford OX4 1JF, England

British Library Cataloguing in Publication Data

Dilman, İlham
    Freud and the mind.
    1. Freud, Sigmund   2. Mind and body
    I. Title
    128'.2'0924   BF173.F85

    ISBN 0-631-13529-4

Typeset by Styleset Limited
Printed in Great Britain by Pitman Press Limited, Bath

Contents

Acknowledgements

I should like to thank the editor of *The Monist* for allowing me to use a substantial part of my paper 'Is the Unconscious a Theoretical Construct?' which appeared in volume 56, no. 3 of that journal — July 1972. This material constitutes chapter 4 of this book.

I am also grateful to my colleague Mr Ian Robinson for allowing me to use some material from my paper 'Freud and Psychological Determinism' which appeared in *The Human World*, no. 11, May 1973. The main part of this material forms part of chapter 11 of this book, although a small part of it has been used in the previous two chapters as well.

Finally I should like to thank Mrs Eileen Wimmers for typing the manuscript.

Introduction

Scope of the Present Inquiry

I believe Freud to have made an original, important and lasting contribution to psychology, one which needs discussion and appreciation. The reasons for this are twofold. First the language in which Freud presents his contribution reflects the philosophical prejudices of his time. It often misrepresents the character of what he was saying and disguises the direction in which he was moving. Secondly, in contemporary popular consciousness, where they get a sympathetic reception, Freud's ideas have lost their depth and are no longer themselves. We cannot, therefore get a balanced view of them there. Nor can we do so if we turn to the academic world for their appraisal. For though they have received a critical appraisal there this criticism has, on the whole, either confined itself to the language in which Freud expressed his ideas, making no great effort to go beneath this surface, or it has itself remained wedded to contemporary philosophical prejudice. Consequently we have to find our own way to Freud's ideas and contribution.

There are three aspects to this contribution: the theoretical or conceptual, the practical or therapeutic, and the social aspects. In this book I am concerned with questions relating to part of Freud's theoretical contribution, that is with some features of his conceptual framework, in particular with questions relating to his conception of the mind and the limits of the individual's autonomy. Thus the scope of the present inquiry encompasses a discussion of Freud's concept of the unconscious, from the point of view both of knowledge and of action, the ways in which Freud thought a person's past may determine his present, the prominence he gave to phantasy and the emotions in his account of human behaviour, the way in which he thought reason and the emotions enter into human actions, his ideas of repression and the divisions of the personality, his conception of self-knowledge, and his views on freedom and determinism.

This inquiry is in fact part of a more comprehensive one of which the first volume has already appeared under the title of *Freud and Human Nature*. There I am concerned with philosophical questions relating to Freud's views on the role of sexuality in human life, his estimate of morality, his conception of the relation between the individual and society, and his notions of character and the emotional development of the individual.

A Controversial Reading of Freud

In these two volumes I develop a way of reading Freud which is in conflict with the popular, orthodox reading of him on the questions I discuss — a reading guided by the surface structure of his thinking, shaped by philosophical presuppositions and prejudices which I criticize. In *Freud and Human Nature* I criticize Freud's hedonistic conception of sexuality and his quasi-mechanistic view of its 'components' and their 'organization', the way he represented the relation between love and sexuality, and between sexuality and the whole person, the kind of universality he attributed to the Oedipus complex, his negative conception of morality as a repressive force, his identification of conscience with the super-ego, the way he opposed human nature and culture, and the terms in which he thought about them, his biological conception of human development through stages of the transformations of the libido, and his exclusive emphasis on the defensive role of character. The popular, and perhaps orthodox, view is that when all this has been criticized Freud is left with no leg on which to stand. My view in the book is that, on the contrary, a critique of all this will clear the way to an appreciation of Freud's real contribution.

The reading with which I replace the orthodox reading of Freud in the present volume can be highlighted under the following headings:

(1) *Non-causal conception of the mind.* I emphasize throughout the book that Freud's mechanistic and causal language stands in the way of a proper appreciation of his aims and achievements. When he speaks of a 'dynamic theory of the mind' what is in question is the prominence he gives to 'inner conflict', 'defence', and 'repression' in his study of the individual's emotional disturbances and behaviour. Central to this study are the individual's aims and motives which divide him in various ways.

So we should not identify what Freud says about 'forces in the mind' with his view of the mind as a cluster of causal mechanisms. In *Freud and Human Nature* I contended that Freud's thinking on the character of man's motives and on the nature of his sexuality should not be identified with the hedonism which I criticize there. I called Freud's hedonism 'philosophical froth'. The same goes for his 'mechanism'.

(2) *Freud's determinism as a vision of man's slavery to a part of himself and the possibility of the individual's liberation from such bondage.* All the same, behind Freud's hedonism there lies a vision of a far-reaching reluctance in human beings to give up certain positions prominent in early life which persist in the unconscious and to which the individual can regress in the face of certain difficulties — among these positions 'the quest for pleasure'. Similarly, while Freud's determinism is shaped by philosophical pre-suppositions regarding the scientific status of psychology and the lawfulness of the workings of the mind, in it we can see Freud's deep-going perception of the extent to which people act in slavery to some part of themselves which they are unwilling to recognize. The philosophical presuppositions obscure the character of this slavery and also turn it into an *inevitable* feature of human life. But as such what is in question is in conflict with the whole rationale of psycho-analysis which aims at liberating the analysand, at enlarging the scope of his freedom. See chapter 10.

(3) *Order in the life of the individual mind, but not general laws.* Even behind the confused idea of the 'lawfulness of

mental phenomena' there lies the idea of their 'meaningfulness', and this is quite independent of Freud's conception of
psychology as a science of the mind. Here too we can discern
something important, namely a vision of the kind of order in
people's lives and behaviour which we should expect a novelist
to exhibit for us rather than a scientist. This line of thinking
too runs counter to the orthodox view of Freud's determinism.
See chapter 9.

(4) *The unconscious mind and the possibility of the enlargement of consciousness*. In his 'justification for the conception
of the unconscious' Freud treated the concept of the unconscious as a 'theoretical concept'. He said that 'consciousness
yields no evidence' for what is unconscious and that we can
only have 'indirect proofs' of it: 'It is an hypothesis – and
science makes use of many.' In this way, just as in some of
his theoretical pronouncements he had turned the yoke under
which he had seen the individual struggle into an inevitable
feature of human life, he similarly turned the difficulties in
'making the unconscious conscious' into an impossibility. I
argue that this is to forget the possibility of an enlargement
of consciousness which is one of the central aims of psycho-
analytic therapy. I do not mean, of course, that this is a
failure of memory on Freud's part or an instance of careless-
ness or clumsy thinking. It is conditioned by the same
Cartesian presuppositions which Freud himself tried to
combat. See chapter 4.

(5) *The enlargement of consciousness as involving a change
in attitude of will and a transformation in the object of consciousness*. I argue that when, for instance, an unconscious
feeling becomes conscious the person does not simply grasp
its indirect expressions. He loses the fear of owning the feeling,
he finds the courage to give it more direct expression, or the
strength to give it up. In either case he stops deceiving himself. It is *he* who gives the feeling direct expression, *he* who
forgoes engaging in evasive activity, *he* who dispenses with
defensive measures, *he* who gives up the feeling. Although
in such a case what was repressed and what is now acknow-
ledged are one and the same feeling, the pattern which constitutes its identity has undergone a change. The change
which constitutes an enlargement of consciousness here is,

therefore, not only in the person's apprehension but also in the expressions in which he apprehends what he feels, the latter being subject to his will within limits. See chapter 4, section 4.

In the case of an unconscious intention this change is a change from bondage to autonomy, so that an unconscious intention is one which a person cannot give up in the normal way. In pursuing it, therefore, he is not an agent in the full sense. See chapter 5, section 3. It is partly in this way that the super-ego differs from conscience in the normal sense of the term. Thus a person who is driven by the dictates of his super-ego cannot be said to do what he wills. In contrast, the actions of someone who may be said to heed his conscience come from him. Such a man is fully behind his actions. See chapter 7, section 5.

These changes are continuous with each other and a consideration of them is important for understanding the connection between the kind of insight sought and the transformation aimed at in psycho-analytic therapy. I would like to explore this connection in a third volume on Freud's contribution: *Insight and Therapy*. There I hope to discuss philosophical questions raised by the practice and aims of psycho-analytic therapy and by the concepts in terms of which Freud thought about and conducted that practice.

(6) *Divisions of the personality and the possibility of an enlargement of the self.* A person's unconscious mind is not *ex hypothesi* unknowable; neither are the divisions between the ego, the id and the super-ego absolute and immutable. What we have here are genuine dissociations within the personality which can be healed.

It is distinctive of Freud's thinking that he saw inner conflict as being at the root of the ills which his psycho-therapy was concerned to remedy. He represented its polarities in different terms, as embedded in 'the structure of the personality', formed in the course of the individual's development, and also as embedded in 'human nature' in the form of instincts pulling the individual in opposite directions. He further regarded the individual as being in conflict with the society which tries to impose its culture on a resisting human nature. The super-ego is that part of the individual which takes the side of society in this conflict while the id represents man's resisting nature. It is only the first of these representations that comes within the purview of the present inquiry. The rest is examined in *Freud and Human Nature*.

Freud froze these conflicts in his theories of instincts and in his conception of human nature and culture as irremediably opposed to each other. Nevertheless, I argue in this book, he regarded 'the structure of the personality' as being modifiable in the sense that the conflicts represented in it can be ameliorated. This is my central contention in chapter 7 and it is crucial for what I say in the rest of the book.

When Freud spoke of the ego as a 'servant' in its relationship with the super-ego and the id he did not mean to deny that it can achieve a position of mastery 'in its own house'. I use the analogy of the relative autonomy of the President of the United States in his relation to his power base to bring out what Freud was denying. I argue that Freud's contribution was to recognize that the ego cannot be master in its own house by the exercise of will-power through repression. Repression is what splits a person, increases inner conflict, curtails his autonomy. Repressing a troublesome emotion or desire is not the same thing as relinquishing it. What one needs to do in order to give it up, turn away from it or grow out of it, is only possible if one can acknowledge and take responsibility for it. That is why Freud thinks of the lifting of repression as a crucial part of what psycho-analytic work needs to achieve. See chapter 6.

If the ego is to be 'master in its own house' it has to put its house in order and be prepared to give as well as to take. This means the 'integration' of the dissociated aspects of the self. Here the person makes his own dissociated inclinations and alien precepts which in the process are modified. Thus the mastery of impulses which lose their impulsive character, and the assimilation of the super-ego by the ego which in the process is transformed into genuine conscience. See chapter 7.

When Freud said that 'the ego is not master in his own house' he obscured these possibilities. Hence the orthodox view that Freud's divisions of the personality are absolute and immutable. Compare with the orthodox view of Freud's determinism. I argue that behind Freud's statement about the ego as a slave to three harsh task masters lies his vision of man's curtailed autonomy.

(7) *Self-knowledge as 'becoming one's best self'.* The orthodox view identifies the enlargement of self-knowledge with the enlargement of consciousness without recognizing that the latter is a change in the person and, therefore, in his disposition of will. I argue that self-knowledge goes beyond this, properly conceived, and encompasses an enlargement of the self, a widening of the domain of one's will. It involves, therefore, the weighing of different modes of evaluation, making some of them one's own, changing or deepening one's relationships with other people, deciding what one wants and so finding who one is. This means taking responsibility for who one is, becoming a person who thinks for himself and is behind what he does. This involves the integration of dissociated aspects of the self and the taking on board of what is new. Coming to self-knowledge or discovering who one is, therefore, is becoming what one was not. It is not only the shedding of screens, but also the integration of what is old and the assmilitation of what is new. See chapter 8, which continues the discussions of chapters 6 and 7.

Structure of the Book

Chapters 6, 7 and 8 form a cluster and they constitute the centre of the discussion of the present book. That discussion is in three 'movements': (a) the unconscious mind and the possibility of a person being deceived about his own mind, (b) the partcipation of the person himself in such deception and the way in which he comes to be divided in himself, and (c) the way in which both self-knowledge and greater freedom is bound up with autonomy and the integration of dissociated aspects of the self as well as its development in its interaction with others. I emphasize how much throughout his discussion of the individual's progress towards greater autonomy Freud underlines the dangers and pitfalls that face the individual. This is of a piece with my emphasis in *Freud and Human Nature* on Freud's conception of the problematic character of individual development and the discussion in

that book of the way we are to understand the importance
Freud attached to the Oedipus complex in that development.
(By 'problematic' I mean 'problem ridden'.)

Chapters 1 to 3 are brief. They are intended to lead up to
the main topic discussed in chapter 4. Only some of the questions introduced in these chapters become prominent in the
later discussion. Thus Freud's idea of psychology as a 'science
of the mind' receives no direct discussion in this book. I discuss the conception of psychology as an experimental science
in a book on Skinner I have now finished — *B. F. Skinner:
A Modern Gorgias — Philosophical Presuppositions in the
History of Psychology*.

There is a secondary theme that runs through chapters 1
to 7, namely a presentation of the changes in the way Freud
thought of the unconscious — from a passive to a progressively
more active conception. What strikes me most in the evolution of Freud's ideas is the way the individual person has
moved to the forefront of Freud's psychology — the shift
of interest from the 'repressed' to the 'unconscious ego',
from 'mechanisms of symptom-formation' to disturbances
of the person, from 'traumatic events' in the past to the
patient's history. The early mechanistic and causal language
of Freud's psychology is, in my opinion, an anachronism,
however much it may linger in some of Freud's later formulations. Hence my contention that Freud's 'mechanism', like
his hedonism, is philosophical froth.

Understanding Freud through a Philosophical Criticism of his Ideas

I believe that the ideas which I discuss here are central to
Freud's conception of the mind. I approach them through
a discussion of the philosophical difficulties they raise. That
is, I try to find my own way to an understanding of Freud's
ideas through philosophy. This is, of course, no substitute
for the kind of experience which can light them up, the kind
of experience which they in turn can illuminate. But though
philosophy is no substitute for this, it can play a role in
bridging the gap between the abstract and the concrete. Thus
when Wisdom's interlocutor complains that under Freud's

chapter headings something is lost, that the general terms used there give a wider but too distant view of reality, so that 'as the detail of the concrete diminishes one loses grasp of what is being talked about', Wisdom suggests that 'the remedy for this is to move to and fro from the concrete, presented by the artist, to the general, presented by the scientist' — or by any other theoretician (1953, p. 261).

Still my treatment of Freud's ideas is critical in the sense that I consider objections to the way Freud thought about the matters he tried to understand. I keep at a certain distance from the language in which Freud expressed himself and do not, I hope, fall into its grooves, swallowing the presuppositions implicit in it. But philosophical criticism, as I understand it, does not imply rejection. It is a search for more adequate ways of expressing an idea — whether it be a philosophical idea or not — provided it has been developed by someone who had something to say. Such criticism must not be afraid to ask what Freud was *trying* to say, to explore the meaning of what he said by reading between the lines. It must not be afraid to search, with the benefit of hindsight, for the direction in which Freud's ideas have evolved, and to see if there is any distinctive pattern to be discerned there.

Most contemporary philosphers would agree that no system of psychology can do justice to the complexity of individual behaviour and to the variety of human motives. Agreeing on this should leave us free to evaluate any such system by the depth of the questions it raises and the penetration of the observations it makes possible.

On this score alone I believe Freud to be the greatest and most original psychologist of this century. He has, almost single-handed, opened up a new way of thinking about men and the problems that beset them in their relationships with each other. Whatever fault we may find with the ways in which he expressed himself, we must admit that he always had something to say.

It is with this that I am primarily concerned: to bring out what he had to say. This is obviously a matter of judgment. But it poses several problems. One that I have already mentioned is the fact that Freud was constantly developing his ideas. The problem here is to sift those trends that are central to his thinking from those that turned out to be dead ends. Another closely connected problem relates to the possibility of distinguishing the 'substance' of what Freud said from the 'form' in which he expressed himself. Some of the ways in which he talked are crude. The question is whether one can intelligibly hold that the crudities belong merely to the expression of his thoughts while in the thoughts themselves he shows a flair for the human heart which we have not yet begun to assimilate. Can what he wanted to say stand up once some of the philosophical presuppositions implicit in it have been discarded? I know the arguments against holding this, but I believe it to be true.

The philosophical difficulties I discuss fall into two groups. First there are those connected with philosophical pre-suppositions that colour Freud's thinking. I see these pre-suppositions as not being essential to what Freud wanted to say and, therefore, as distorting the expression he gives to his insight, disguising it from us. Here I try to cut through the surface and to exhibit Freud's contribution to the questions I discuss. I don't defend what Freud says; I argue that it does not do justice to his insight. Hence my controversial reading of Freud. Secondly, there are the philosophical difficulties raised by those concepts of Freud which need to be kept, not rejected. Here the resolution of these difficulties helps us to appreciate the concepts and to gain a better understanding of what Freud wanted to say by means of these concepts. My conclusion here is that we should not let the philosophical difficulties lead us to reject what Freud says. Thus in the case of the former difficulties I turn away from the 'manifest content' of Freud's thinking, and in the case of the latter ones I attempt to remove 'philosophical resistance' to its acceptance.

It is in this way that the philosophical discussion in this book is part of a search for Freud's insight. But it is only part of it in two ways. First because of the limitation of its scope which I have indicated earlier. Secondly because there can be no full appreciation of Freud's insight without a struggle to gain it in oneself. If psycho-analysis is *one* way of attempting to be honest with oneself and of taking a dispassionate view of one's past, then one would have to admit that it encourages self-criticism much in the spirit in which Socrates advocated it. The relation between such self-criticism and the kind of criticism that is central to philosophy is a topic for investigation. I said, '*If* psycho-analysis is one way of attempting to be honest with oneself', and I know that this has been denied. It has been said that psycho-analysis is a form of persuasion or indoctrination. I do not believe that it need be so, but this is another claim that will have to await consideration.

1

Freud's Discovery
of the Unconscious

1   A Conceptual Innovation

In the first chapter of *An Autobiographical Study* Freud
gives an account of how he arrived at the idea that 'there
could be powerful mental processes which nevertheless
remained hidden from the consciousness of men' (1948b,
p. 29).

He had formed the resolution to study under Charcot and
was able to do so in 1885 when he was appointed Lecturer
in Neuropathology. In Freud's presence Charcot demonstrated
that hysterical symptoms — paralyses and contractures — can
be produced by hypnotic suggestion. Freud writes: 'Such
artificial products showed, down to their smallest details, the
same features as spontaneous attacks, which were often
brought on traumatically' (1948b, pp. 21–2). Together with
other visitors Freud was astonished and sceptical, and tried to
justify his doubts 'by an appeal to one of the theories of the
day'. But this conflict with established theory did not disturb
Charcot. On one occasion he said to Freud: 'Ça n'empêche
pas d'exister.'[1] Freud writes that these words left an indelible
mark upon his mind. He was to find himself many times in
the same situation.

The fact that hysterical symptoms can be produced by
hypnotic suggestion turned Freud's interest to the *psychology*
of the neuroses — although Charcot, himself, took no special

---

[1] It is true despite theories to the contrary. Compare with Galileo: 'eppur si
muove' — all the same the earth does move.

interest in penetrating more deeply into this psychology
(1948b, p. 23). Two ideas were forming themselves in Freud's
mind: (a) that the source of these symptoms may be not so
much in the nervous system as in the patient's mind, in his
thoughts and feelings; (b) that perhaps these thoughts and
feelings are not accessible to the patient himself.

Later, in 1889, after setting up a private practice in Vienna,
in which he treated hysterical patients largely by means of
hypnotic suggestion, he travelled to Nancy in France and
spent several weeks there, looking for ways of improving his
methods of hypnosis. There he was a spectator to Bernheim's
astonishing experiments with his hospital patients, from
which he 'received the profoundest impression of the possibility that there could be powerful mental processes which
nevertheless remained hidden from the consciousness of men'
(1948b, p. 29).

So we have two facts: that hysterical conditions can be (a)
produced or induced, and (b) removed by hypnotic suggestion.
In both cases the subject is unable to remember and so is
unaware of the suggestion to which he responds. Add to
these the following two facts. (c) Freud had heard from
Breuer, a family physician and neurologist in Vienna, even
before he went to Paris, of a girl, Anna O., who, under hypnosis, recalled events from her earlier life which she could not
recall under normal circumstances (see Freud and Breuer,
1950, case history I). (d) The events in question were invested
with a great deal of emotion and recalling them under hypnosis cleared the symptoms. So, in a paper 'On Hysterical
Mechanisms', Freud writes that 'hysterical patients suffer
principally from reminiscences' (1950, vol. 1, p. 29; or Freud
and Breuer 1950, ch. 1, p. 4). The reminiscences are beyond
recall, except under hypnosis.

What impressed Freud most of all was the analogy he saw
between the facts of hynosis and the phenomena of hysteria.
It made him look at the symptoms and conduct of his patients
from a new angle and he saw them in a new light. He writes
of a patient:

Mental processes had been at work in her and the obsessional
action was the effect of them; she had been aware of this effect

in a normal fashion, but none of the mental predeterminants of this effect came to the knowledge of her consciousness. She behaved in precisely the same way as an hypnotised subject whom Bernheim had ordered to open an umbrella in the hospital ward five minutes after he woke up. The man carried out this instruction when he was awake, but he could produce no motive for his action. It is a state of affairs of this sort that we have before our eyes when we speak of the existence of unconscious mental processes. (1949a, p. 234)

This little phrase 'in the same way' indicates part of what lies at the kernel of Freud's discovery of the unconscious. He reasoned that the puzzling behaviour of his patients too may come from 'ideas' which they had kept in their minds for a long time. They denied having such 'ideas' and yet quite spontaneously gave expression to them under hypnosis. Freud reasoned that they must find these 'ideas' painful. The fact that similar behaviour could be induced by hypnosis further confirmed him in his conviction that at the root of hysterical symptoms and obsessional behaviour lie unconscious 'ideas' — memories, thoughts, wishes.

This means that Freud spoke of 'ideas', e.g. memories, where previously we would not have spoken of them. We could say that in developing the above analogy Freud modified the use of some familiar terms. Professor Wisdom, who pointed out that 'a person's understanding grows only as his ability to carry out comparisons grows' remarked that 'psychoanalysts in order to reveal to us things about ourselves modify and sophisticate our conceptions of love, hate, jealousy, envy, sympathy, sense of responsibility. They use familiar words not with a disregard of established usage but not in bondage to it' (1953, p. 271). Where the boundaries of a concept's application are widened it is given a greater power to mark certain connections, affinities and continuities which, in its previous use, had remained unmarked. This is a gain — 'a gain in meaning and connection' (Freud, 1950, vol. iv, p. 99). However, it acquires this power at the expense of its power to mark differences and discontinuities which it previously marked, and in so doing served us well. This is a loss. So long as one does not forget these differences, or extend the boundaries until they disappear, one will have gained something and lost nothing. Critics have accused Freud of doing both these things. We shall see later what justice there is in these charges.

I have so far mentioned three interrelated aspects of what constitutes Freud's discovery of the unconscious.

(1) He opened our minds to the possibility of distinguishing between appearance and reality in the mental world. He was convinced that a person could really have a thought or desire, be haunted by a memory, and not recognize this.

(2) It became clear to him that when this is so, the person himself is opposed to the recognition. He is unwilling to face the desire or memory and avoids doing so. Here Freud talked of 'repression' and used the word 'resistance' where the person engages in frustrating any attempt to bring this to his attention.

(3) Freud was further struck by the way the 'contents' of a person's unconscious mind remain immune from considerations that otherwise weigh with him. Thus a memory may remain alive over a period of years, though unacknowledged, unaffected by the intervening passage of time and whatever may have occurred in the course of it — e.g. the unconscious memory of an insult in the past under which a person still smarts.

(4) In refusing to equate appearance with reality in the mental world Freud altered our vision of the shifting contents of consciousness. He enabled us to think of some of these shifts as more apparent than real. He enabled us to represent what appears to us as something new or an aberration as something that has been with us or part of us all along. As Jung puts it: 'We are like those primitives who believe that every evening the sun dies and vanishes, and that if anything rises next morning, it is a new sun' (1940, p. 11). Referring to the aftermath of an experience of emotional transport, he went on: 'When the storm has blown over, and the former self has appeared again, we prefer to think that the whole thing has not been true. Yet nothing of this kind really disappears. It merely returns to the unconscious, where it awaits its next opportunity. For a keen eye, even, it does not disappear completely. Its influence is still there, less obvious, yet more subtle and cunning' (pp. 20—1). We could say that

Freud developed the conception of the unconscious and with it presented a greater continuity in the mind.

(5) In his paper 'The Unconscious' Freud wrote: 'Unconscious processes can only be observed by us under the conditions of dreaming and of neurosis; that is to say, when the processes of the higher system Pcs revert to an earlier level by a certain process of degradation (regression)' (1950, vol. iv, p. 120). The word 'process' here is a misnomer. Freud has in mind the kind of *mentality* or mode of thinking that gains the upper hand in times of mental breakdown when stress defeats a person's normal ways of dealing with difficulties, and also during sleep in our dreams. By 'unconscious processes' he means the kind of thinking that is characteristic of the unconscious mind, one that is imbued with phantasy and is relatively impervious to reason. (For a discussion of some of the questions this raises see chapter 3 below.) In his biography of Freud, Ernest Jones rates this as the most important aspect of what constitutes Freud's discovery of the unconscious: 'Freud's revolutionary contribution to psychology was not so much his demonstrating the existence of an unconscious, and perhaps not even his exploration of its contents, as his proposition that there are two fundamentally different kinds of mental processes, which he termed primary and secondary respectively, together with his description of them' (Jones, 1954, p. 436).

Both the expressions of this mentality and the extent to which people deceive themselves about their own feelings and thoughts had been recognized before and portrayed by great novelists and dramatists — Proust and Dostoyevsky for instance. Freud, himself, acknowledges this. On his seventieth birthday he said: 'The poets and philosophers before me discovered the unconscious. What I discovered was the scientific method by which the unconscious can be studied.' What literary writers produced were penetrating portrayals of imaginary cases based on their experiences in real life. Freud, on the other hand, developed a method, that of free association in a controlled clinical setting, in which the impressions conveyed by these portrayals were substantiated. He further ordered this knowledge in a particular way. The point of view he developed in doing so was revolutionary in its application to psychiatry. It yielded new insight in his case studies. In this way Freud was able to test his point of view in practice, see what it is worth, in a way which it is not the business of imaginative writers to do.

This is what I take Freud to have meant when he said that before him the existence of the unconscious had been mainly a matter of speculation and that he was the first person to put it on a scientific footing. It doesn't mean that reflection did not have an important role to play in the way Freud innovated our conception of the mind. It did — as it does in the development of any major scientific idea. However, though connected with clinical experience in the way I suggested, Freud's innovation was not connected with experiments in the way that Galileo's and Newton's discoveries were. For it is a discovery within the field of our knowledge of human beings. And the fact that human beings are capable of lying and deception, as well as of trust and sincerity, is obviously relevant to the character of this knowledge. So is the fact that the very being of the feelings and thoughts to which they give expression in their speech and behaviour presupposes the circumstances of human life. There is little here that we can abstract from these circumstances in the way required by experimental methods. The kind of knowledge in question can, therefore, only grow in the course of human intercourse and its verification requires contact with an alien will. In short, the application of experimental techniques is founded on abstraction, manipulation and observation; but the furthering of clinical knowledge involves attention to particular details in their natural setting and human intercourse or interaction. (See Dilman, 1975, pp. 205—9, and 1977, section 2, pp. 45—50.)

Freud, himself, recognized this. In one of his *Introductory Lectures* he says that while psychiatry is interested in conditions common to given states or symptoms, psycho-analysis, in contrast, is interested in individual history: 'Psychiatry . . . in pointing to heredity gives us a general and remote aetiology instead of first disclosing the more specific and immediate one' (1949a, p. 216). He points out that the 'meaning' of neurotic symptoms appears in the history of the individual and cannot be seen in abstraction from this (p. 218). In

Studies in Hysteria introducing his discussion of the case of
Elisabeth von R. he writes: 'I still find it a very strange thing
that the case histories I describe read like short stories and
lack, so to speak, the serious imprint of science . . . In the
study of hysteria . . . an exhaustive account of mental processes, of the kind we are accustomed to having from imaginative writers, enables me to obtain insight into the origin of
hysteria' (Freud and Breuer, 1950, p. 114).

'Lack the serious imprint of science': this makes it sound
like a defect. I have suggested that Freud's comment is directed
to the character of our knowledge of human beings. It does
not imply that there cannot be a serious study of human
beings, but that such a study cannot take the form of an
experimental investigation. Still this does not mean that it
has no foundation in experience, or that it is mere speculation.

I have tried to point out that Freud's discovery of the
unconscious has different aspects and that although it is
founded on clinical experience it is largely *conceptual* in
character. It is not in this respect that it differs from Galileo's
and Newton's discoveries. For at the core of their discoveries
too lie conceptual innovations. This is what Wisdom (1953,
p. 253) wished to emphasize when he said that with the word
'gravity' Newton connected occurrences that had seemed
disparate and 'presented the power of the distant', as with
the concept of the unconscious Freud 'presented the power
of the past'. Thus what Freud put forward was not an hypothesis but a framework of ideas in which hypotheses are
formulated and checked, predictions are made and confirmed,
new facts surmised and discovered, explanations offered and
justified. He provided a way of representing and co-ordinating
a range of facts. He suggested the possibility of treating these
in new ways, changed our understanding of them, and encouraged us to anticipate new facts.

Ernst Mach said that 'physics lives and grows by comparison'. To make a new comparison, to see a new resemblance,
means seeing one thing in the light of another thing, and so
seeing it 'under a new aspect'. This may enrich our vision of
it, deepen our understanding. When this is so, the perception
of an unsuspected analogy which suggests a new mode of

representation will amount to a *discovery*. Is this true in the case of Freud's innovation?

I don't think that we can consider it in isolation from his other innovations. The analogy that had struck Freud when he witnessed the 'experiments' of Charcot and Bernheim was a bolt of lightning. If it lighted up much for him, that is because his mind was already occupied with and full of questions on the subject. From it he took his start and continued to develop his idea of the unconscious mind in connection with other ideas. In the rest of the book, and in the other two mentioned in the Introduction, I hope to consider where this led Freud, whether it was a fruitful path, and whether it bypassed other turnings and as a result impoverished our understanding of certain aspects of human life.

2   'The Unconscious': Merely a Collective Noun?

In a piece entitled 'Fact and Hypothesis' Dr Drury refers to the facts of hypnosis I mentioned earlier. He says: 'They are facts which the language of everyday life is not equipped to describe except in terms of a long circumlocution. So it became convenient to introduce a special terminology and to speak of "unconscious" memories and "unconscious" motives. But every adjective is in deadly danger of being transformed into a substantive. So it came about that psychologists began to speak of "the unconscious mind" as if some new *entity* had been discovered' (1974, p. 138). Drury speaks here of the danger of imagining that 'the unconscious mind' is a 'mysterious second self' which accompanies us at all times and is the 'real' source of what we do and suffer.

The unconscious mind is, of course, not some new entity, just as the conscious mind is not some old or familiar entity. For the mind is not an entity at all; and neither is the discovery of the unconscious like the discovery of a new continent. Yet insofar as Freud treated the affirmation of its existence as the assertion of the truth of an hypothesis he helped to encourage the 'superstition' which Drury opposes: 'A man may be ignorant of many things. Together they make

up the things he is ignorant of or does not know. If we refer
to these as "the ignored" or "the unknown" we shall simply
be using a collective noun. If we now attribute a special power
to what the noun refers to or names, as Groddeck does when
he writes that "man is animated by the unknown" (1950,
p. 16), we shall be inclined to think of it as something that
acts on man, directs what he does and determines what he
suffers. In doing so we shall have fallen a prey to a mythology
created by our way of speaking.' These are not Drury's
words, but something like what they say was in his mind
when he wrote the words I quoted from 'Fact and Hypothesis'.

Drury is right, and yet his warning may limit our understanding. We do talk of a person's 'mind', meaning sometimes to comment on his intelligence, sometimes on his
emotions, depending on the context of the conversation, and
our talk presupposes a certain kind of unity in what we are
referring to, even though this is not the unity of a substance.
Could this not be equally true when we talk of a person's
'unconscious mind'? The unity here lies in the continuity
of the memories, beliefs and intentions that pull his activities
towards a centre. We are certainly not referring to a substance or entity named 'the unconscious' over and above the
unconscious memories, emotions and intentions we have in
mind, but we mean to give prominence to their interconnec-
tions, so that we can speak of the man as acting from a centre
he does not himself recognize and, therefore, with restricted
autonomy.

What is of interest is the possibility of a person being
active when he seems to be the passive recipient of incidents
that leave their mark on his life. This activity is an additional
dimension to his conscious activities which he does not
recognize and cannot be fully at one with. He may, for
instance, pursue unconscious strategies which occupy a
prominent position in his life, so that a good deal of what he
does and suffers can be claimed to be partly at its service. If
this makes sense, a question I shall consider further on (see
chapter 5 below), then can we not speak of an unconscious
aspect of his personality, in conflict with his conscious
personality as defined by his avowed aims, conscious interests
and purposes? My point is that there is more to talk of 'the

unconscious' — to using the substantive instead of the adjectival or adverbial forms — than confusion and mythology. What is unconscious is not simply what we are ignorant of or deceived about. The noun is meant to cover aspects of ourselves to which we stand in a special relation — memories that haunt us, intentions that we form, policies we pursue, grudges to which we cling, chips on our shoulders, our resentments and sulkings. There may be sufficient unity between some of these things, sufficient continuity in time, to make 'the unconscious' more than a collective noun, to justify us in regarding what it refers to as something which has a positive power over the individual. But when we so regard it, we should not forget that what drives him in a certain direction, what frustrates the pursuit of his conscious goals, is an aspect of the agent himself.

2

Unconscious Memory:
the Power of the Past

In a symposium entitled 'Is the Conception of the Unconscious of Value in Psychology?' Professors Field and Laird objected to the way Freud talked of 'the exciting experience continuing in some way to be effective even years after . . . directly as the actual exciting cause'. Field wrote:

> What I want to know is why the effect which the event produced on the person should be described as if the original event somehow went on existing and working? . . . We do not think it necessary to talk like that in any other connection. Many events in this physical world produce permanent results beyond themselves. But we do not, except very figuratively, speak of the event as continuing to exist or as going on happening somewhere. Nor, indeed, would it really be intelligible to do so. An event, whether in the physical world or in conscious experience, when it has once happened is over and finished. It is not in any sense a thing in itself with a permanent existence and a capacity for different kinds of action. When an event produces a result, the result is something other than itself and cannot be described in terms which imply the continued existence of the event which caused the result. (1922, p. 416)

He argued that all we need to talk of here is a 'permanent disposition or tendency' established in the past. Similarly Laird said:

> The past event to which we return in memory . . . is over and done with when we look back at it, and it remains over and done with however frequently we look back at it . . . Although these

events have consequences for our subsequent history, it is non-sense to say that they persist. (1922, p. 422)

This is obviously true in many cases of memory and know-ledge. A man has witnessed an occurrence two weeks ago. We say the he knows what happened then, that he hasn't for-gotten. We mean that he can tell us now if we ask him. There is no suggestion that he carries a mental image with him from which he reproduces the account of what he witnessed. Even if we wish to speak of a 'mnemic trace' and think of it as a modification in the brain cells, this is still a 'permanent result', one that succeeds the past perception. It is at best a causal condition necessary to the remembering of what was winessed. What the man does between then and now is independent of his memory, unless he actually thinks about the event in question.

'He hasn't forgotten' may mean two different things; we use the expression in two different cases. We use it, as above, to mean that he *can* describe or do certain things. Thus we may say that he hasn't forgotten the lessons he learned as a child. But we also say of a man who still grieves for the wife he has lost three years ago that he hasn't forgotten her. We say of the man who served a prison sentence for a crime he committed that he hasn't forgotten what he did. We refer to the repentance that characterizes much of what he does. The idea of what he did is implicit in his present repentance and, therefore, in much of what he does. This is what we mean when we say that he hasn't forgotten.

The memory in these two cases is fully conscious. We could say that his wife is constantly in his thoughts, that the idea of what he did is ever present in his mind. Of course we do not mean anything like a process going on in his con-sciousness — like the man who can think of nothing else because he is in pain all the time. But if this is what the expressions, 'she is constantly in his thoughts', 'the idea is ever present in his mind' mean, then they could apply to a person who denies what they claim about him. He leaves his wife for a more exciting life. Later he is seen in a new place, shunning old friends, and changing the subject whenever anything connected with his wife comes up in conversation.

He is often heard to exalt the richness of his present life. Yet to a few sympathetic friends he appears restless, unable to settle down. Can we not imagine a particular way of filling in the surrounding details so that it would be true to say that he has not been able to forget his wife, that he cannot get her out of his mind?

The grieving man in our earlier example gives himself to the memory of his dead wife and, loving her as he does, he embraces what that memory demands of him. The man who has left his wife, on the other hand, fights her memory and refuses to give in to what it exacts from him. Instead of missing her and recognizing the error of his present life he clings to it. In fighting that memory, in not allowing himself to miss his wife, he is fighting himself. This is one reason why he cannot make much of his present life, and why the memory of his wife haunts him. It stands to reason: the man who will not pay his debtors will not be free of them.

Take another example. A young man grows up to fear the father who beat him in his childhood. That situation may have changed now, but the fear continues. It permeates his present relationship with his father and spills over the rest of his life. What confronts him in his father now is a figure from his childhood, stronger than he is and bent on imposing his will on the son. He sees his father as he saw him long ago and feels himself as he did then. If today he responds submissively this is not simply because his past experiences have moulded him into a submissive person. He is not simply acting from permanent dispositions instilled in him by experiences long finished and gone — as Field thinks. He is responding to an ongoing situation that is alive in his memory.

It was this kind of possibility that Freud had in mind when, at the early time of his collaboration with Breuer, he said that in hysteria the patient suffers from reminiscences. Here the whole ambiance of a past traumatic experience has remained alive in the patient's memory to haunt him in his present life. Yet it cannot be exorcised so long as he fights it and does not know he is doing so. Fighting it is a way of clinging to it. Thus Freud thought of hysterical patients as 'ghost-ridden'. This is the forerunner of his later ideas of 'fixation', 'regression', 'transference' and 'repetition-compulsion'. These belong as much with Freud's concept of the unconscious as his ideas of 'repression', 'defence' and 'resistance'.

At first Freud thought of 'traumatic experiences' as rooted in real events which the patient had suffered in his childhood. When he later came to see that he had little justification for supposing that such events as his patients recounted had really taken place, he came to think that they must have imagined them. This brought into prominence the role in the patient's present life of certain 'ideas' from his childhood and his part in their formation. It is, therefore, not a backward step in the development of psycho-analytic theory, as some of Freud's critics have claimed, an attempt to cling to a pet hypothesis in the face of adverse evidence by reducing its claims, but a forward one. It is a change in conceptual orientation, one which the present chapter is concerned to understand.

I said that the son in my previous example continues to see his father as he saw him long ago. Hence his submissiveness. But the harshness and severity feared in the father may have been a reflection of his own unfriendly feelings of jealousy, a reflection of the way he would himself have liked to have acted. His fear may thus have been a fear that his father would retaliate in kind. In this kind of case Freud speaks of the son's vision of his father and of his worst expectations as a 'phantasy'. Such phantasies presuppose the framework of family relationships as we know them, although the means employed in their construction belong to an archaic mentality.

Once the idea of such phantasies became prominent in Freud's thinking his early conception of trauma began to fade into the background. For what became important was the patient's contribution to his early relationships, what he made of them, and the early emotional situations in which he got caught up. What began to impress Freud more and more was the extent to which the patient lived and acted out these early situations in his present life. He said that the patient repeats these patterns without being able to recall the situations in which they originated. Insofar as they find a foothold in current situations and relationships with figures in his present life Freud spoke of 'transference'. He said: 'The transference is overcome by showing the patient that his feelings do not originate in the current situation, and do not really concern the person of the physician, but that he is reproducing something that had happened to him long ago. In this way we require him to transform his *repetition* into *recollection.* Then the transference which . . . seemed the greatest menace to the cure becomes its best instrument, so that with its help we can unlock the closed doors in the soul' (1949a, p. 371). These words were spoken twenty years or so after the publication of *Studies in Hysteria* and gives expression to a different conception of what brings about the cure of a neurosis. At present I am not interested in this. I quote the passage because it illustrates my point about Freud's conception of the power which the past, frozen in the unconscious, exerts on the patient's present life. Field and Laird show no understanding of this.

When I say 'frozen in the unconscious' I am thinking of the kind of 'repetition' that is an expression of 'unconscious memory' in the sense under discussion. It has to be contrasted with 'habit memory' which has no idea-content and can be analysed in terms of 'permanent dispositions' formed in the past in the way Field suggests. For what characterizes it is a pursuit of ghosts from the past which one is unable to exorcise because one will not recognize them. Freud became aware of such ghosts in his own life during his self-analysis, though he was not able to exorcise them, and he wrote about them with penetration in *The Interpretation of Dreams*. Speaking of a dream about Brutus and Caesar he wrote:

Strangely enough, I once did play the part of Brutus. When I was a boy of fourteen, I presented the scene between Brutus and Caesar in Schiller's poem to an audience of children, with the assistance of my nephew, who was a year older than I, and who had come to us from England . . . Until the end of my third year we had been inseparable; we had loved each other and fought each other, and . . . this childish relation has determined all my later feelings in my intercourse with persons of my own age. My nephew John has since then had many incarnations, which have revivified first one and then another aspect of a character that is ineradicably fixed in my unconscious memory. (1967, p. 460)

Again

> My present . . . annoyance . . . draws reinforcements from springs
> that flow far beneath the surface, and so swells to a stream of
> hostile impulses towards persons who are in reality dear to me.
> The source which furnishes the reinforcement is to be found in
> my childhood. I have already said that my warm friendships as
> well as my enmities with persons of my own age go back to my
> childish relations to my nephew who was a year older than I. In
> these he had the upper hand, and I learned how to defend myself
> . . . In a certain sense, all my friends are incarnations of the first
> figure; they are all *revenants* [ghosts]. My nephew himself returned
> when a young man, and then we were like Caesar and Brutus. An
> intimate friend and a hated enemy have always been indispensable
> to my emotional life. I have always been able to create them
> anew . . . (1967, pp. 520–1)

There are many different ways in which what a person
came into contact with and lived through in the past makes
a difference to the way he develops and influences what he
becomes in the future. There are also different senses in
which a person may be said to be the same as he was before.
Whether what he meets in his childhood contributes to his
development or arrests it, it will have influenced what becomes of the child in the future. This is one of the dividing
lines for Freud relevant to his concept of repetition — what
Proust calls 'the plagiarism of oneself'. But there are difficulties in understanding what 'arrest' means in this connection —
as there is not if we are speaking of the body being stunted
by lack of nourishment. Putting these aside for the time
being,[1] we could say that what Freud has in mind is the case
where an experience so affects a growing child that it blocks
the possibility of something new entering his life from a particular direction. The contrast is with the case where the
child learns from what he meets or experiences. He acquires
something which stands him in good stead in the future,
something which enables him to meet new situations differently.

---

[1] I return to these in Dilman, 1983, chapters 7 and 8.

Where a child's development suffers an arrest, whatever he meets seems to give out the same echo, so that relatively little that is new comes into his emotional life. He gets older and learns many of the things which his contemporaries learn, but he continues to fight his childhood battles in the new circumstances of his adult life, to defend himself against the same dangers which pursue him into his grown-up life. I shall give two examples, though they are *not* examples of arrested development. For the first I refer to an aspect of Freud's own life to which he draws attention in *The Interpretation of Dreams*:

> When I was seven or eight years of age another domestic incident occurred which I remember very well. One evening, before going to bed, I had disregarded the dictates of discretion and had satisfied my needs in my parents' bedroom, and in their presence. Reprimanding me for this delinquency, my father remarked: 'That boy will never amount to anything.' This must have been a terrible affront to my ambitions, for allusions to this scene recur again and again in my dreams, and are constantly coupled with enumerations of my accomplishments and successes, as though I wanted to say: 'You see, I have amounted to something after all.' (1967, p. 250)

As one of his biographers comments: 'This single evidence of paternal rejection was sufficient to haunt him all his life . . . His single-minded pursuit of greatness and achievement all through his life . . . was an effort to vindicate himself in the eyes of his father' (Puner, 1959, p. 43). There is no reductionism in this comment with which Freud would have agreed. What is claimed is *not* that his achievement was 'nothing but' an effort to vindicate himself. It drew its energy from many other sources, not least from a genuine interest in the questions he investigated. The point is that Freud had not got the early humiliation described above out of his system, so that much that occupied him in later life retained a reference to it. Because the humiliation remained with him he continued to react to it, and in doing so he kept it alive.

My second example concerns the life of the writer Anthony Trollope, about which the psycho-analyst Dr Harry Guntrip makes some perceptive comments in his book *Healing the*

Sick Mind. He is thinking about the way Trollope's childhood remained active in his adult life, influencing it for the good:

> A friend of his mother was daughter-in-law to the head of the G.P.O. and begged a clerkship for Anthony. Though the first seven years were misery, his application for the post in Ireland opened out a new life for him, a life of constant travel usually on horseback which he loved. He developed a passionate attachment to the work of improving communications for isolated districts and lonely people, and there is no doubt that the driving force of his devotion to his work was a symbolic compensation for his own early loneliness *which still survived in his deepest feelings.* (1964, p. 200; italics mine)

It is not denied here that Trollope was genuinely interested in his work and cared about the loneliness of people living in isolated districts. On the contrary, it is suggested that his own childhood experiences made it easier for him to understand the plight of these people, to feel for them and want to improve their situation. But it is suggested that his pursuits to alleviate their loneliness was at the same time a pursuit to redress something in his own childhood which had remained alive in his feelings and which he saw reflected in the plight of these people. Guntrip brings out well how experiences earlier than those of Trollope's school days and adolescence *sustained* him through his wretchedness and loneliness, so that he did not grow bitter and retained the desire to make things good. This is what enabled him to take a genuine interest in the plight of those who reminded him of his own early wretchedness, an interest strong enough for him to want to improve it.

Guntrip comments further down:

> There remained in the personality of the successful adult Anthony Trollope some features that betrayed the presence of unresolved internal conflicts. He presented the typical combination of aggressiveness masking a deep need for love . . .
>
> He was still fighting for a place among his school fellows in his deepest feelings, still struggling to prove himself to be somebody . . . The experience of being an utter nobody as a child was there to be compensated to the end. One of his late-attempted but unrealised ambitions was to be an M.P., as a 'conservative

liberal', motivated particularly by the pain it caused him to observe the cruel inequalities of fortune among men. (pp. 204—5)

This need for compensation was not self-centred, for it
merged with the desire to make things good. This, in turn,
derived from earlier experiences of a good relationship with
his mother as a child, before he went to school, one which
remained alive in his feelings throughout his life. Without it,
I imagine, it would have been easy for him to feel deprived
and envious, easy for his need to prove himself to become
self-centred, and for him to find little sustenance in the love
and affection he later found in the woman who became his
wife.

Both examples are 'mixed cases'. For although in both
there is a single-minded return to the same thing, what Freud
and Trollope bring to it enables them to make something new
of it and thus something by which they are enriched. This
too has its source in childhood and is the love which Trollope
received from his mother. But its mode of survival in Trollope's
later life is different from Freud's memory of his father's
words or Trollope's memory of the wretchedness of his
school days.

I said that Trollope's good relations with his mother
'remained alive in his feelings throughout his life'. This is not
an instance of 'repetition'. For it is not something to which
Trollope kept returning in later life, something to which he
clung. It is on the other side of the dividing line I mentioned
earlier. It is something that enables him to grow, something
that contributes to his development. It enables him to find
something new in what he meets, not just a reverberation of
his past life, and so both to give and receive, and to be transformed in the process. It is not something that he keeps alive,
something that could be said to 'haunt' him. The sense in
which it remains with him, the sense in which he may be said
to have retained it, thus keeping in touch with his past, is
different from the sense in which his early conflicts remained
with him. Compare the latter with the sense in which someone may be said to have grown up with a chip on his shoulder,
to have continued to nurse old grudges. Where a person can
derive sustenance from his past there is nothing 'frozen'

about such a past. Here if we say 'he hasn't forgotten the love his mother gave him, or the kindness of an old teacher', we are contrasting him with someone who turns his back on his past and repudiates what he was given.

Obviously both gratitude and resentment for something that happened in the past involves memory. Yet the way in which the past remains alive for the grateful person and the way it does so for the resentful one are very different. The former can be said to have 'kept in touch' with it. In gratitude what he has received becomes truly his. The latter 'dwells' on a past incident, he cannot turn his mind away. For it to let him go he will have to forgive what he feels to be an injustice. Such forgiving is a change in him. In forgiveness what was 'frozen' thaws and becomes mobile again. The energies and interests trapped in conducting a feud become available for a more 'productive' interaction with the environment — I mean one that involves greater give and take. Obviously if there is to be any forgiving the resentful person will have to recover the memory of what he has continued to resent over the years. In contrast, in the case of the grateful person, there is no logical room for talk of an unconscious memory. For there is nothing that he continues to act out and nothing that he fights remembering.

If we say of someone that he was aggressive as a child and that he is still as aggressive, that he has not changed in this respect, we are not referring to anything that *goes on*. What is in question is a mode of response that is the same now as it was in his childhood. It is different if we say that he is 'still fighting for a place among his school fellows'. In the latter case we are saying more than that he responds to different situations in the same way. We are claiming that his response is determined by certain ideas that are independent of the situations that evoke it, ideas from which the person cannot turn his mind away. It is through these ideas that the past in which they were formed shapes the present in its own likeness. He is not just permanently disposed to respond to certain situations in a particular way; he continues to act out the same battles or conflicts irrespective of the circumstances. This is the kind of perpetuation of the past which the notion of unconscious memory is meant to bring into focus.

3

Unconscious Phantasy: Reason and Emotion

In *An Autobiographic Study* Freud speaks of 'the large extent to which psycho-analysis coincides with the philosophy of Schopenhauer' and, in enumerating the respects in which it does so, he mentions 'the dominance of the emotions' (1948b, pp. 109—10). Elsewhere he says: 'Psychoanalysis unhesitatingly ascribes the primacy in mental life to affective processes, and it reveals an unexpected amount of affective disturbance and blinding of the intellect in normal no less than in sick people' (1957, p. 175).

This is directly connected with the prominence Freud gave to the part which 'primary processes' play in our mental life, those same 'processes' which 'can only be observed by us under the conditions of dreaming and of neurosis'. What Freud has in mind is a particular kind of mentality — determined by the emotions and dating back to early childhood before the growth of judgment and autonomy. Obviously a person has to learn much before the modes of action and apprehension that belong to adult life can become his. Only then can he share its interests, meet its problems, engage in the kind of thinking and reasoning with which people respond to these. Freud's view is that while people do genuinely grow out of this early mentality, they do not outgrow it completely. It remains with them, though disowned, to constitute a 'background to their conscious mental activity'. When it breaks through into consciousness it 'stands out in the crudest contrast to the rest of the conscious mind' (1950, vol. iv, p. 105).

Freud has in mind the way emotions from early childhood, such as greed and envy, the desire to control others or to prove one's worth, can enter into sophisticated ambitions, such as those of a scientist engaged in a new piece of research, and exert influence on the thoughts and aspirations that give them content. He has in mind the way our reactions to disappointments, difficulties, losses and victories, to demands made on us and challenges that come our way, may have their roots in situation we met earlier in life, at which time the ideas that give content to our present reactions would not have been intelligible to us. He is thinking, in short, of the way our present reactions may contain emotions which animated those earlier reactions. Yet from the perspective of the ideas that give content to our present disappointments or victories, to the demands and challenges that face us in our current life, it is not easy to see how these earlier emotions and ideas can find a home in our present reactions. The frame of mind to which they belong remains alien to our conscious intentions and preoccupations, worries and hopes.

Let me put it differently. In understanding a person's response to a particular situation we have to take account of its significance, as he sees it, and of the kind of person he is — his desires, interests, values, fears and apprehensions. This significance is assessed, as Hume would say, by reason, in terms of the relevant concepts and categories which the person has acquired through education and interaction with others in the course of activities belonging to the culture of his society. In Freud's view, this significance is not exhausted by what one may call its 'public face'. There is another dimension to it: that of unconscious phantasy. For, on this view, we do not live wholly in the world of common sense, where what we meet, take an interest in, desire and pursue, fight or run away from, is understood in terms of the categories with which we think and reason about it. Most of the things that engage our interests, desires and emotions have another face which affects us equally, even though we may be unaware of it. It goes against the grain of the main emphasis of our whole education to try to put it into words — although some literary writers have done so.

By a 'mentality' I mean a way of thinking about things,

one which determines the aspects of things that count for us. When I speak of an adult mentality, as we are familiar with it in our culture, I mean a mentality in which categories of reason, such as 'cause and effect', 'ends and means', 'validity' and 'evidence', occupy a prominent position. In contrast, the mentality which belongs to the unconscious is dominated by phantasy. It finds direct expression in dreams, in moments of stress, frustration and mental exhaustion. We may also be able to allow direct expression to it by deliberately suspending the exercise of our critical faculties.[1] Hence the 'method of free-association' used by psycho-analysis to investigate the unconscious mind.

Consider an example. An artist has always maintained that criticism has an important role to play in the development of artistic ideas. His own work is subjected to adverse criticism and he loses sight of what he has always preached and believed. He tells himself that the criticism is fair and has at heart a concern for the art to which he has been contributing; but he cannot help thinking of it as hostile and directed against his person. He feels slighted and hurt. But worse, the criticism seems to spell out annihilation for him and fills him with panic. An outsider may try to explain his dismay and depression by saying that they are a measure of the depth of his concern for his art. But for this to be true we would have to imagine that the criticism reveals to him some poverty or defect in his work. But this need not be the case; he may have very high standards and never fool himself where his art is concerned.

If our artist imagines some 'personal animus' behind the criticism, this need not be a piece of self-deception, even if it is untrue. The fact that he takes it this way is indicative of phantasies which in no way reflect on the genuineness of his interest in his work. Perhaps the criticism is not fair minded, perhaps it does really come from envy. Others in his place would dismiss it for just that reason. If he is unable to do so, may this not be because his art has become a prop to his identity, because it has become a mirror in which he loves

---

[1] A thing not easy to do; one which the way we have been brought up and our deeper fears militate against.

himself? If so, is it any wonder that he finds it imperative that it should be flawless? Is it any wonder that anyone who faults it threatens him at the same time? Freud would go further and wonder: if he did not feel vulnerable in his identity as an autonomous person, would our artist read so much significance into the adverse criticism he has received? If this diagnosis is correct, then the phantasy that he is nothing if what he produces is no good, is part of a whole field of phantasy rooted in early situations. In one such situation, for instance, he may have wanted to give something to his mother and he may have interpreted her lack of appreciation as a total rejection. Freud's claim is that such situations from early childhood, as he saw them at the time, may continue to exist in his feeling, colouring those that he meets in adult life. But phantasy here does not mean fiction.

It is, of course, possible that to our artist's phantasies of annihilation there corresponds complementary phantasies in the critic. But even if this is true and the criticism does come from a level of animosity rich in omnipotent phantasies of destruction, it does not in reality annihilate the artist. What does annihilate him, in the sense in which he fears it, is his own *belief* that he has been annihilated. For in the life of phantasy there is no distinction between thought and reality. In believing that his work is rotten he does really lose the prop on which he has been leaning.

We could say of our artist that he thinks that an unfavourable word has the power to destroy him, just as the hero of Proust's novel, Marcel, has the idea that a kiss from his mother could restore him to life. We find such ideas contrary to reason, and so those who have such ideas find it difficult to acknowledge them. We dismiss them as irreconcilable with our rationality and are, therefore, unable to spell out their content. Phantasies are what give content to such ideas and they have their origin in early childhood relationships of dependence in which a single word or gesture of rejection is tantamount to annihilation. The kind of reason which in adult life makes us dismiss such an idea as preposterous was not accessible to us at the time and, certainly, we had to learn much before we could think otherwise. One could say that phantasy, in this sense, is the original element of those relationships in which the significance of what takes place is determined by our emotions, the bodily needs with which these are bound up, and the expectations conditioned by them. Proust describes Marcel's despair as a young child when his mother, detained by guests, is unable to come up to his room as usual to kiss him good night. This despair, he says, was later to 'migrate' into his later loves, giving them their peculiar feverishness. The despair is about being nothing without the confirming response of the beloved. It drives Marcel to want to possess the beloved, and each failure leaves him exposed to the original despair.

What thus 'migrates' into a person's later relationships, his interests and preoccupations, are constellations of feeling, the contents of which are rudimentary thoughts and expectations which originally found expression in his emotional reactions as a child. It is these thoughts and expectations which Freud and Melanie Klein call phantasies. We could say that phantasies are what a person comes to think and do in his imagination as a result of what he feels. Whether he is active or passive, the emotion gives credence to the thought or imagination, so that he believes what he thinks to be the case, is convinced that what he has done in his imagination has really come to pass. Thus we say that 'in his feelings' she has left him. Perhaps she has just gone out with a friend or expressed some pleasure at the prospect of doing so. Although he knows that this does not mean that she no longer cares for him and enjoys his company, there is a part of him which cannot believe it. He grieves and feels dejected.

We say that 'in his imagination' he has debased her, meaning that he has thought of her in denigrating terms. Of course, the fact that he has done so may show him something about what is happening to his relationship, or about what is happening to him morally in that relationship, and he may be distressed by what he sees. To understand his distress we have to refer to his moral beliefs, not his phantasies. Thus contrast, 'He has begun to look down on her' and 'In his imagination he has debased her'. In the latter case his guilt and distress has a more primitive content. He sees her as debased and blames himself for her condition. In the converse case we say that 'in his imagination' he has elevated her. This is an instance of 'idealization' and is to be contrasted with looking up to or admiring someone.

'In Othello's feelings Desdemona had been unfaithful to him and had betrayed his love for her.' We mean more than that he believed it and so felt betrayed. Iago did not merely deceive him by telling him an untruth. He had discovered a sore spot in Othello, a weakness, a vulnerability, and he played on it for his own purposes. What he told Othello produced conviction not through reason, but through feeling. Othello did not believe Iago because he had reason to trust him or had no reason for distrusting him. Something in him was disposed to believe what he heard.[2] We may speak here of a predisposition to believe, as we speak of a preconception. A person who has a preconception approaches facts with a closed mind. Similarly one who has a predisposition to believe something responds to what he is told with his mind already made up. It is not the reasons in favour of what he is told that bring about his conviction, since reasons against it are powerless to dissuade him. The predisposition to believe lies in what he feels. This is the credence conferred by the emotion on the judgment implicit in it. We could say that 'jealousy believes in the inconstancy of its object'. Thus Othello was not jealous of Desdemona because he came to believe her to have been unfaithful; he came to believe this when Iago succeeded in arousing his jealousy. Being the kind of man he was, jealousy was an inherent part of the kind of love he had for Desdemona, a love at once possessive and exacting, idealizing and mistrustful. Iago, sensitive to this weakness, simply provided the pretext whereby what was in Othello's feelings would find a foothold.

The idealization and the mistrust that characterize Othello's love for Desdemona are opposite yet complementary aspects of that love. He did not mistrust Desdemona because she had

[2] Thus compare the way Iago's words work on Othello with the way a psychoanalytic interpretation works on the patient. Freud might have said that Iago's words were true at the level of 'psychic reality'. In other words, in Othello's phantasy the woman for whom Desdemona stood proxy had betrayed Othello by taking her love elsewhere. Though Iago was lying to Othello at the level of everyday life – as a psycho-analyst would not – and he had ulterior motives, nevertheless at *this* level he was speaking the truth.

ever let him down. The defect was not in her, but in him.
What he lacked was a belief in the constancy of women — a
capacity to hold on to such a belief. Yet he needed to relate
himself to a woman who would comfort him, one he could
come back to and who would make him whole again (see
Act I, scene 3). For this it was essential that he should be
able to believe in her constancy. So what he was deprived of
in the way he felt he made up for in phantasy: in idealizating
the woman of his love. It was this defensive idealization that
Iago attacked. Its collapse revealed a flaw in his idea of the
woman he loved. This idea, in turn, was sustained by his
feelings. Thus we have a passive phantasy: what in his feelings
was true about the object of his love, namely her inconstancy.
And we have a secondary active phantasy: what he did in his
imagination to remedy this state of affairs, namely his idealization of her.

I have contrasted 'conviction through feeling' and 'conviction by reason' and I suggested that the former mode of
conviction belongs to the realm of phantasy. I am not, of
course, speaking of emotions in general, but only of those
that involve 'regression' in their mode of conduct and awareness. Sartre (1948) has written perceptively about these in his
Esquisse d'une Théorie des Émotions. What, after Husserl, he
calls the 'intentionality' of emotions is well recognized by
Anglo-Saxon philosophers. What has not been recognized by
them is the way emotions can transform or, as Proust would
say, 'metamorphose' their object — invest it with what Sartre
calls 'magical' qualities. As he puts it: 'Being terrible is a
property of this Japanese mask' (1947, pp. 33–4). Sartre is
not merely saying that when we describe the mask as 'terrible'
we do not mean that it inspires terror in us, but we attribute
a property to it. His point is that the category of the terrible
belongs to the emotions, that the property we attribute to
the mask is a denizen of the world of the emotions, of magic
or phantasy, one that is the antithesis of reason.

Sartre means that our reactions to things seen as having
such properties are not determined by reason. Thus,
presumably, when we come upon a snake we know to be
poisonous from its markings and we are afraid of it, our
response is governed by reason. If we discover that these

markings are not those of a poisonous snake our fear vanishes. The significance of the markings which was the basis of our fear can be understood in terms of the categories of inductive reason. It is well known, however, that some people's fear of snakes goes far beyond the effects of their venom. The fact that they crawl and wriggle, are slippery and cold-blooded, is the sort of thing that gives them a menacing aspect. It does so by touching a chord that is more resonant in some people than in others. But what gives a thing that has these characteristics a menacing aspect? To answer this question one would have to bring before one's mind images conjured up by snakes. And here one may consider examples from literature, legends and fairy stories, which draw on our phantasy life and express fears to which most of us are susceptible. Similarly for the terrifying aspect of the Japanese mask. Here it is connections with images of cruelty, ruthlessness and violence, and facial expressions embodying them that give them the aspect which Sartre has in mind.

There is, obviously, a difference between seeing the mask as terrible and being terrified by it — even though these are closely connected. Thus imagine suddenly seeing a face in the dark, pressed against your window pane. Or imagine seeing the shadow of a tree moving in the moonlight as you wake up in bed, still in a state of semi-slumber. It looks eerie, strangely menacing, and you are terrified for a moment until you are fully awake. You then see the moving shadow for what it is, its terrifying aspect disappears. Why were you so afraid? What did you think it was? It was not because you mistook it for something dangerous that you were terrified. It was because the image it conjured up gave it a menacing aspect. Not being fully awake you were in a state of suggestibility, vulnerable to phantasy, and the distance that normally separates you from the things you see had dropped out. In your feelings you were wholly at its mercy. Sartre would say that the aspect under which you saw the moving shadow has no equivalent in the world of common sense — the world of instruments used for certain purposes, of objects with specific causal properties. In T.S. Eliot's words: it has no 'objective correlative'. In the example of the face pressed against the window pane what you saw caught you unawares, off your stride. For a moment you forgot where you were. The familiar landscape of your thinking slipped away. It was replaced by a landscape of the kind with which we are familiar in dreams.

Convictions that are thus determined by the emotions are not amenable to reason. For what evokes such an emotion does not coincide with what we may try to reason about. Our reason may tell us that the insect from which we shrink away is harmless and will not bite or sting us. But this is not why we cannot bring ourselves to touch or handle it, and so we continue to find it creepy and repulsive. Why can we not bring ourself to touch something creepy, why do we shrink away from it in revulsion? There are no further reasons that we can give. We can at best try to illustrate the significance which creepiness has for us, what we mean when we describe something as 'creepy'. We surround the images we have produced with comments, remark on their connections, in the hope that our reaction will become intelligible. It will become so in the end only if what we say strikes a chord in other people, if it connects with the phantasy-life we share with them.

I was asked why I found the moving shadow menacing? In what way menacing? In the sober light of the day I cannot see. I have to turn that light down, to transport myself imaginatively into the frame of mind in which I was at the time: can I articulate the thoughts that gave content to my terror? Can I let the fear I felt then speak for itself? If I could, I might find out that what I was afraid of was that the shadow would envelop me and take over. It was this malevolent intention that I had read into its eerie aspect, into its sinister movement.

Such phantasies are in terms of categories immediately accessible to a child. The ideas of good and evil in them are those we find in children's stories and fairy tales. They are closely related to elementary pleasures, desires and fears. The phantasies are almost wholly made up of images of the body, its functions, processes, products and elementary actions involving these: tearing, biting, hitting, stroking, cuddling, sucking, swallowing up, spitting out, breaking up, putting together, etc., and their passive counterparts. It was Freud's view, and later Melanie Klein's, that these are among the earliest categories of the young child's thinking — those that enter into his understanding of what is happening to him, inside and around him, and into his longings and fears. The child, at this time, has as yet hardly learned to act on his environment, to seek the fulfilment of his wishes by communicating them in terms intelligible to others, to make use of relations that exist independently of his thoughts to obtain what he wants. His body-centred needs and desires find expression in movements and reactions which he has not yet learned to direct, check or control. The capacity to form and pursue intentions, to stick to them in the face of obstacles, the capacity to entertain, examine and hold beliefs on the basis of evidence, are capacities that develop in the child in the course of his interaction with those around and close to him, especially his parents, through what he learns from them. All this transforms the infant's life and world fundamentally. His emotional life becomes much richer and acquires many new dimensions, and the terms of his childhood phantasies can come nowhere near to doing justice to this richness. We could say that it becomes potentially as rich as the life of the society to which he belongs, with its art, its literature, its rituals, its complex conventions and their meaning. Entering the life of such a society, sharing its interests, facing its problems, makes him capable of having feelings and desires he could not have had otherwise. The relationships into which he enters have dimensions which his early childhood relationships could not have had, dimensions which go far beyond the scope of his early phantasies. If so, how could these phantasies have the scope and significance in his adult life which Freud and Melanie Klein attribute to them?

Freud's view is that we do not altogether give up thinking in these categories, that something of this mode of thinking survives this gradual but fundamental change in us and influences our response to certain situations and the direction of our interests. This influence becomes more direct and obvious when a person's normal way of coping with stress, frustration or conflict breaks down. For then these earlier modes of thought and behaviour take over. As Susan Isaacs, a colleague of Melanie Klein, puts it: 'Unconscious phantasies exert a continuous influence throughout life, both in normal and neurotic people, the difference lying in the specific character of the dominant phantasies' (1952, p. 112).

When I asked how these phantasies can be claimed to have the scope and significance attributed to them I was raising a philosophical question: If we are to steer clear of any form of reductionism, would we be left with anything that can be salvaged in Freud's view? I believe there is a great deal that can be salvaged. Let us consider an example. A man who cares for literature finds himself drawn into a controversy in the columns of a paper. Positions become polarized and in one of the letters he writes he ridicules the view he is opposing, by implication showing its holder in a denigrating light. One could say, and truly, that his passion is an expression of the deep feeling he has for literature. We could not understand what literature means to him without understanding the diverse aspects of life which it is capable of portraying and the role which such portrayal has in our lives. The passion that has been aroused in our correspondent is bound up with his appreciation of this and with his commitment and concern. No one who lacks this appreciation can share his passion.

This much may be perfectly true in our particular case. But there may be more to the story, a possible way of developing it which does not detract from the genuineness of what our correspondent feels for literature. Why does the other man's shallowness anger and exasperate him so? I answered: because by what he says he cheapens what our correspondent cares for. This answer is complete in itself and leaves nothing unintelligible about the caustic tone of his letter. The emphasis in this response may be on protecting something valued or on attacking those who debase it. In the former case there will not be much animosity. In the latter case there is a greater scope for the conflict to become personalized. The venom it may then draw out of the opponents may still be couched in sophisticated phrases and terms of righteous indignation. In the case of our correspondent this will be a return of the missile he feels has been hurled at him or 'his side'. This missile has the power to attract his phantasies.

We can then say that his perfectly genuine passion for literature draws him into a situation which brings out a response in him from a different level of his personality. This gets intermeshed with the one inspired by his concern for literature. There is always this possibility that anything which evokes a deep response in us may touch less mature aspects of our personality. These will then intrude and may distort the original response. Freud's claim is *not* that our *prima facie* understanding of the man's engagement and response is suspect or incomplete, but that often there is *more* to his response than we make of it. Whether or not we are interested in this depends on the questions we wish to raise.

The stand our correspondent takes in his letters, the passion he puts into them, all this is inspired by his concern for literature, and there cannot be any counterpart, in his early life, to the pattern of meanings which makes this concern intelligible. Yet there is a continuity of development between the aspect of his personality that is engaged in this stand and the aspect that is dragged into it through regression. To the regressive aspect the stand is something much less lofty, what engages his emotions is something much more personalized, and the demons which draw out his antagonism are much less differentiated than those internal to his concern for literature. It is to the extent that this aspect of his personality enters into his response that phantasy becomes relevant to it.

In 'Feeling and Expression' Hampshire pleads for combining a 'genetic' with an 'analytical' approach to the elucidation of mental concepts. He argues that 'in the particular case of feeling, the inner life of the mind is to be understood as a development from something more primitive in every man's behaviour, of which it is the residue and the shadow' (1961, p. 8). This inner life is a dimension which a child's life gradually acquires as he learns to identify his emotions and inclinations, to put them into words and, thereby, to control them. This is made possible by these emotions and inclinations having 'natural expressions' which are in the first place 'constitutive' of the emotions and inclinations themselves. Thus in the case of anger, for instance, Hampshire refers to 'a disposition to attack when the subject has been, or believes to have been, in some way harmed or hurt' (pp. 8–9). The two capacities to identify and to control our inclinations develop together as we learn to speak and to reflect on ourselves and our circumstances. The use of language in the communication of emotions and the inhibition of the actions they prompt are learned in harness. The 'successive stages of the interiorisation of feeling' correspond to the successive stages of the control of the impulsive behaviour originally constitutive of the emotions we were subject to as children. The bodily expressions of emotions — posture, gestures, facial expressions — and the feelings are residues of the original behaviour. Thus, in the case of anger, a scowl or a shaking of clenched fists is a 'truncated action'.

This is a very condensed version of one strand in Hampshire's argument. Let me link it with the present topic under discussion. Acquiring language necessarily brings with it an extension in the range of what as children we wanted to have and do, and with it an extension in the range of the inclinations at the centre of our emotions. This means an extension both of what can rouse emotions in us and of what our feelings amount to on these occasions. As adults we are capable of emotions which we could not have had as children. But alongside this vast *qualitative change* in our affective life we must also recognize an *historical continuity* between the earlier and later stages of our development. Hence what Hampshire characterizes as 'residues' of the behaviour that belongs to the earlier stages — e.g. the shaking of clenched fists, the showing of teeth in a snarl. The unconscious phantasies I have spoken of belong with the actions and reactions which are truncated in these gestures and expressions, and they survive in the form of metaphors in sophisticated language.

No reductionism is suggested here of the diverse forms of emotion to their earlier stereotypes. All that is claimed is that there is a genetic continuity between them which constitutes a life-line along which the earlier forms exert some influence on the responses inspired by their later varieties. This influence may be benign or vicious. Thus in the above example I said that our correspondent's response may be primarily a stand for something he believes in and cares for, or it may be a retaliatory attack. I commented on its 'aggressive' aspect. Let me comment, briefly, on its aspect as a stand for something cherished. Here the way he cherishes the literary values which have been attacked in the columns of the paper and the character of the stand he takes will reveal what he has in him to give. Does he need any glory to sustain him in his stand? How dependent is he on external support or encouragement? Surely the way he has developed in the course of his early interactions with his parents and in his later friendships will determine, at least partly, the character of his response to what is asked of him here, how he rises up to it, as well as what he makes of it, what he considers to be at stake. Once more it is possible, though not necessary, for his tenacity to be fed by images of devotion dating back to his childhood and relating to his parents. This would be an instance of what I meant by the benign influence of early phantasies. I have touched on this earlier in my comments on the example of Anthony Trollope (see chapter 2 above).

4

'Unconscious Mind': a Contradiction in Terms?

1   *Is What Is Unconscious* Ex Hypothesi *Unknowable?*

I characterized Freud's discovery of the unconscious as 'conceptual' and denied that what he advanced was an hypothesis. I was not thinking of the kind of discovery that a patient may make about himself in analysis when he realizes that his feelings are different from what they seemed to him, or that he has desires which he condemns in others. These are unconscious feelings and desires, his own, and the interpretations that help him to recognize them may be tentative and advanced as hypotheses. But they need not be, and they can be directly confirmed.

Freud must have known this in his practice. But when he stopped to ask what grounds there could be for assuming the existence of the unconscious, it seemed to him that whatever grounds there are must be indirect: 'An unconscious conception or idea is one of which we are not aware, but the existence of which we are nevertheless ready to admit on account of other proofs or signs' (1950, vol. iv, p. 23). So he says that 'consciousness yields no evidence' of what is unconscious (p. 99). Otherwise what is unconscious would not be unconscious.

But this is a muddle. If someone may be said to have an unconscious wish to hurt a friend this means that he has such a wish but is not aware of having it. There is, however,

nothing to prevent him from becoming aware of this —
except, of course, his own reluctance. What he cannot do is
to be aware of the wish while the wish can be correctly
described as 'unconscious'. This is a harmless tautology, as
harmless as the tautology that one cannot see something that
is concealed from sight while it is so concealed. It does not
follow, however, that what is concealed at one time cannot
be seen at another time.

Why, then, do we think that there can be no direct knowledge of the unconscious? Why are we inclined to pass from
the harmless truism that a person cannot know he has a wish,
e.g. to hurt someone, *while the wish is unconscious*, i.e. concealed from him, to the falsehood that he cannot *ever* know
he has it? The answer, briefly, is that we think that there can
be no change where the mind is concerned, no change from
ignorance to knowledge, no change in consciousness, which is
not a change in the identity of what the man wishes. The idea
is that there can be no distinction between the reality or
identity of a wish or feeling and the subject's consciousness
of it, in other words that this consciousness constitutes the
wish or feeling in question. This is the Cartesian identification of mind with consciousness which Freud referred to as
'the first shibboleth of psycho-analysis' (1949b, p. 10).

Freud thought not only that the person himself cannot
have knowledge of his own unconscious mind, but also that
no one else can do so: 'By the medium of consciousness each
of us becomes aware only of his own state of mind' (1950,
vol. iv, p. 101). When, however, his friend and colleague
Fliess took him at his word Freud was annoyed: 'You take
sides against me and tell me that "the thought-reader merely
reads his own thoughts into other people", which deprives
my work of all its value' (1954a, letter 145). Yet, though
he repudiated this form of scepticism, Freud could not make
a clean breast of it: 'That another man possesses consciousness
is a conclusion drawn by analogy from the utterances and
actions we perceive him to make, and it is drawn in order
that this behaviour of his may become intelligible to us ...
The assumption of a consciousness in him rests upon an
inference and cannot share the direct certainty we have of
our own consciousness' (1950, vol. iv, pp. 101—2). He took

this to be as true of the 'assumption' of unconscious thoughts and feelings in other people.

These two sources of difficulty combine to encourage the idea that what is unconscious is *ex hypothesi* unknowable. This idea took firmer root in Freud's thinking when he compared our position with regard to the unconscious with our position with regard to material objects which, he thought, can only be known indirectly. He was further misled by Kant's distinction between appearance and reality and by his suggestion that we cannot know things as they are in themselves: 'In psycho-analysis there is no choice for us but to declare mental processes to be in themselves unconscious, and to compare the perception of them by consciousness with the perception of the outside world through the sense-organs' (1950, vol. iv, p. 104).

From this it is a small step to the idea that the existence of the unconscious is a theoretical assumption: 'It is an hypothesis and science makes use of many' (1947, p. 14). 'The index-value of the unconscious has far outgrown its importance as a property' (1950, vol. iv, p. 29).

In this way sources of philosophical confusion forced Freud to conclusions which contravened his own perceptions and weakened his treatment of the philosophical criticisms which he wished to rebut. Obviously, he did not wish to deny that patients in analysis can become aware of aspects of their own minds which form part of their unconscious. In fact he described the aim of interpretation in psycho-analysis as 'making the unconscious conscious'. We shall examine what this transformation amounts to in section 4 below. But to appreciate that such a transformation is *possible* we have to clear up the sources of confusion I have just mentioned. I shall concentrate on the first of these.[1]

2   *Consciousness and the Mental*

Contrast the concepts of a physical reality and an hallucination or mental image. When I say that there is a dagger

---

[1] I have examined the second, namely scepticism about one's knowledge of other people's minds, elsewhere. See Dilman, 1975, Part II.

before me, and I am not lying or joking, then it could still be the case that there is no such thing there. Cameras, other people, my inability to clutch it, perhaps its sudden disappearance, may force me to admit that I was mistaken. If I had said, 'It *seems* to me there is a dagger before me', then none of this, nor anything else, could force me to amend or withdraw my statement. As Descartes puts it: 'Even if no imagined object is real, yet the power of imagination really exists and goes to make up my experience. These objects are unreal, for I am asleep, but at least I seem to see, to hear, to be warmed. This cannot be unreal' (1954, pp. 70—1). That is, nothing can prove these to be unreal or illusory. Nothing can show me to be mistaken as far as they are concerned.

Descartes then goes on to say that what makes this so also necessarily makes the objects in question *mental*: 'And this [namely what cannot be unreal or illusory, what I cannot be mistaken about] is what is properly called my sensation; further, sensation, precisely so regarded, is nothing but an act of consciousness.' In other words, when I say, 'Hot!' I am speaking about the weather if I am willing to amend or withdraw what I said on the basis of what thermometers read, how other people look, and what they say they feel. If I am not willing to do so on any such basis then I am not speaking about the weather but about how I feel. What makes my words incorrigible here is the very feature which makes them words about how I feel. Again, when I say, 'There's a dagger before me', if I allow cameras, other people, my other senses, and the future to prove me mistaken, then I am speaking about a real, physical dagger. If, on the other hand, I am using these words in such a way that nothing of this can prove me mistaken, then I am speaking about a 'dagger of the mind', an hallucination, a mental image.

But is Descartes right? May not a statement or report be open to the challenge of the future and that of other people and still be a statement about the mind? Of course it may. Words like 'I feel depressed, angry, jealous' are often so used as to be predictive and, therefore, open to the challenge of the future. They describe patterns which recur 'in the weave of our life — with different variations' (Wittgenstein, 1963, p. 174). Wisdom speaks of them as 'subtle patterns in time' which may be 'hard to grasp' and which 'cannot be covered at a glance' (1953, p. 274). So even when there is a sufficient stretch for the pattern to be recognizable one may still fail to take it in.

Are the words we are concerned with also open to the challenge of other people? Let us take an easy case. I say that I love a certain woman. Later I say that I thought I loved her but now I see that I did not. Where I make two such reports about an after-image I see the latter report cannot constitute a correction of the former one — or rather it can do so only in a limited sense.[2] But with love the situation is different. For my present thought that I did not love her, when I thought and said I did, does have a basis which other people can share. I can intelligibly ask, 'Was I right then when I thought I loved her or am I right now when I think I did not?' This is a question which other people can help me to answer. There are criteria independent of my thoughts which anyone can use to answer it, criteria for deciding the identity of my past and present thought. So I can say that my thought, apprehension or consciousness has changed, but not its object, namely my feeling for her. I can say that these are what they have always been, although they no longer seem to me what they seemed when I first knew her. This is to be contrasted with the case where I say I have stopped loving her, where my feelings have changed.

When I say that I never loved her, that I was mistaken when I thought I did, I rely on my memory. But what is it that I remember? A great deal of it is what other people can remember equally well: my behaviour at the time, the flowers I took her, the promises I made, the various things I said, the circumstances of our relation. It may also include a memory of flutters and sensations and sinking feelings I had at the time. Here other people will remember my words which they may or may not have reason to doubt. But I am not now casting any doubt on these words when I say

---

[2] In some cases we would take the latter report as a correction and find it natural to do so. But if the person who thus changes his mind were to oscillate between the two reports, it would be meaningless to ask which one gives the true description of his after-image.

that I have come to realize that I never loved her. Today, perhaps in the light of what I remember followed them, in the light of my present experience, I no longer attach the significance that I attached to them at the time.

In those cases where the flutter I feel in my heart convinces me that I am in love my knowledge is indirect, dependent on past experience (see Wisdom, 1952, p. 121). Also what I am convinced of has a certain complexity that may make it difficult for me or another person to appreciate what it amounts to. Hence there is room here for both inference and reflection. As Wittgenstein puts it: 'It makes sense to ask: "Do I really love her or am I only pretending to myself?" and the process of introspection is the calling up of memories, of imagined possible situations, and of the feelings that one would have if . . . ' (1963, section 587). Reflection, or introspection as it is called when it has one's own actions, motives, and feelings as its object, takes the form of recollecting what one felt like, what one said, did and thought, of using one's imagination, making predictions, trying to see connections, comparing one's behaviour and circumstances with those of other people, real and imaginary. This form of reflection is open to other people, provided one is willing to talk to them frankly and without reservation. (For a fuller version of what I have argued so far in this section, see Dilman, 1972, section 3, pp. 320–5).

It is because his conception of everything mental was modelled on the logic of sensations and mental images that Descartes identified what is mental with consciousness, claiming that if it *seems* to a person that he is afraid, angry or in love, that he has this inclination or that desire, then it must *really* be so. Its *seeming* to him that he is afraid, for instance, is what he would express as 'I am afraid' or 'I feel afraid'. For Descartes this means, 'I am in a certain state of consciousness', so that the words, 'I am afraid', are an expression of the speaker's state of consciousness. This state of consciousness *is* his fear. It follows that such fear cannot exist apart from the particular state of consciousness, and equally that the state of consciousness cannot exist when the person is not afraid. It is at one and the same time the person's fear and his introspective awareness of the fear. This rules

out the possibility of an unconscious fear or other emotion.
It also rules out the possibility of false emotions that hide a
person's true affective disposition, a disposition which would
have to be characterized as unconscious.

Now if fear were a sensation, if it were a mental state constituted by the here and now of consciousness, in the way
that Descartes imagined, then indeed a person could not be
afraid and not know that he was, nor could he think he was
afraid when he was not. But we have seen that what makes
it true that a person is afraid of something are not his sensations of the moment, the sensations that characterize his
consciousness at the moment. Fear characterizes a person's
consciousness in an altogether different way, his consciousness of the object to which he is responding. If, for instance,
he really fears an imminent confrontation with someone, a
rival let us say, then this fear is the form which his consciousness or anticipation of that confrontation takes, the terms in
which he thinks of it, his affective response to it. The state of
consciousness which takes this form is directed to the object
of his attention and response, namely the dreaded confrontation. What gives it the particular character it has, the one we
designate as 'fear', is not a matter of what goes on in him at
the time. It is his relation to the imminent confrontation,
which is what it is by virtue of what has preceded the present
moment and what will come after it, and also the circumstances that surround his present thoughts, sensations and inclinations.

This is itself a possible object of reflection, and the way it
strikes him, the way if figures in his consciousness, may be
quite different from the way he anticipates the confrontation
in reality. The content of his consciousness and what he really
feels need not coincide. It may seem to him that he is confident
and without fear when in fact the opposite is the case. Alter-
natively, the fear which the thought of the confrontation
seems to evoke in him may be part of the way he misrepresents
to himself his response to it. In reality his attitude may not
be one of timidity but one of aggressiveness, and the fear
which the confrontation evokes in him in his anticipation
may not be, as he thinks, a fear of his adversary. It may be

a fear of what he imagines he might do to his adversary. It may thus hide his aggressive phantasies and inclinations.

So it is both the idea of consciousness and that of what is mental that we misapprehend, as Descartes did, when we identify the two and think of an unconscious emotion or inclination as a contradiction in terms. Consciousness is not the stuff that constitutes what is mental, whether it be an emotion or inclination. Rather it is the person's apprehension of whatever it is he is concerned with or affected by. It may be explicit in his thoughts or implicit in his responses — in his distress at what has happened, his guilt about what he has done, his pleasure at or fear of what he anticipates, his attraction by someone or interest in something. These are forms of consciousness of things.

Equally, a person's own responses, his emotions and inclinations, can be the object of his consciousness. Here too his consciousness of them is very often unreflective. He may apprehend them correctly or misapprehend them. In the latter case they take a distorted form in his consciousness, they take on an appearance there which is different from what they are. Where the discrepancy between appearance and reality is great we could rightly say that he has no consciousness or awareness of, for instance, the way he feels. In other words, his feelings do not figure in his consciousness, he takes no cognisance of them and even, perhaps, actively avoids doing so, as often happens in life. This is where Freud speaks of the feelings and emotions in question as unconscious.

So much for the side of consciousness. As for its objects, the feelings and emotions in question, I have argued that their reality or existence is a matter of the person's relation to their objects, the significance these have for him, the way they touch or affect him. The latter embraces his thoughts, actions and responses, the actions he takes, the responses he controls or contains, and also the bodily, somatic reactions which he experiences as sensations and bodily feelings. It is these, taken as a whole, which Wisdom refers to as 'patterns in time'. Obviously what pattern they constitute depends on the particular surroundings or circumstances of the person's life.

The sensations and bodily feelings in question are the mental counterpart of his somatic reactions, and their mental registration is a form of consciousness that is not directed to anything. It would make no sense to assert their existence and deny that the person was conscious of them. But they are only an element of the pattern and their significance is subject to the place they have in the pattern. They contribute to the pattern certainly, but only as the notes in a melody contribute to the melody. As we know well, we hear the same notes differently in different formations, sequences or melodies. Similarly, a flutter in the heart may be an expression of excitement or a symptom of fear.

It should be clear that if emotions such as fear, anxiety, guilt, depression, anger, envy are complex patterns in time, they may figure in our consciousness in many different ways. We need not necessarily recognize them in ourselves. The content of our consciousness need not coincide with what we feel; what we take our feelings to be in what we experience, however compellingly, may be very wide of the mark.

3   A Person's Final Say on what he Feels or Desires

It remains true that, whether we recognize them or not, the patterns in question are constituted partly by our active responses, by our attempts to make sense of the things to which we respond, and partly by our passivities, by what we suffer, our somatic reactions and bodily feelings. We are related to both aspects of these patterns in a special way. To speak in the first person, the responses are *mine*, the significance which their object has for me is subject to my scrutiny — it is not simply something given. I thus enter into the patterns in question as a person with various capacities. Even when there is little I can do about the course which their development takes I am not related to them as a bystander. I can at least endorse or repudiate them.

As for those aspects of the patterns which are passivities, they are still *mine* in the sense that I am the one who suffers them. My relation to them is different from that of anyone else. Thus if I were a patient in analysis and my analyst suggested that my cheerfulness was a manic defence and that underneath this exterior I was feeling very depressed, my relation to what the analyst interprets would be very different from the analyst's relation to it. As Freud puts it: 'A consciousness of which its possessor knows nothing is something very different from that of another person' (1950, vol. iv, p. 103).

This has two consequences. The first is that whether or not I take cognisance of the depression, and acknowledge it, is ultimately up to me. It is up to me in a special way to which I shall return in the following section. The second consequence is epistemological in character and it is this. While I fail or refuse to recognize the state of depression in which someone else sees me to be, while I do not acknowledge that depression, the grounds which justify him in claiming that I feel depressed will not and cannot be what they would be if I were to acknowledge it. This is a tautology. What is not a tautology is that in that case there would inevitably be an element of conjecture in what he claims. The only thing that would remove this element would be my acknowledgement of what he claims, of what he says I feel. And I can only do so when I become conscious of the depression I feel. This is because of the special relation in which I stand to what I acknowledge. For when I say, 'I feel depressed', this is not simply an expression of assessment on my part: it is itself an expression of what I feel.

This is the ground which the other person, my analyst, lacks when he offers an 'interpretation' of what I feel. Yet this is not just one kind of ground among others. It has a special epistemological position. As Professor Malcolm puts it: 'The testimony that people give us about their intentions, plans, hopes, worries, thoughts, and feelings is by far the most important source of information we have about them' (1977, p. 102).

Malcolm's point is that such first person utterances as 'I intended to keep my appointment' and 'I am annoyed' are often our criterion of what the person in question intended or felt: 'We use this testimony as a new criterion of what he is feeling and thinking, over and above and even in conflict with the behavioural criteria' (p. 101). However, this does not mean that we can never question this testimony. We can have reason in a particular case for thinking or suspecting that the person giving it is insincere or self-deceived.

It remains true, nevertheless, that if we have grounds for doubting a person's testimony about his intentions or feelings in a particular case, there are many cases where we have no such grounds, and even where we would find a doubt unintelligible. The possibility of reflecting about another person's situation, words and behaviour with a view to forming a judgment about his feelings, hopes, motives and intentions presupposes that there are circumstances where we are prepared to take people's testimony about themselves at face value and not meet it with doubt or suspicion. If, one way or another, such testimony can be deceptive in one situation, or even in a whole series of situations, this is because there are circumstances in which we regard them as reliable and beyond question.

Still each time I have a person's testimony I have to use my judgment. Can I take what he tells me at its face value? Where I can do so there is no further question for me as to whether he really thinks what he says he thinks, or whether he really feels what he seems to feel, judging from the way he behaves. These are the situations in which Malcom would say that the *criteria* of someone's having such-and-such a thought or feeling are satisfied. If, on the other hand, I have reason to think that I should not take his words or behaviour at their face value, then I will have both to reflect on his words and behaviour now as well as on other occasions and also talk to him. It is important that I should talk to him and not merely observe him.

There are at least two reasons for this.[3] First, a great many things that one may wish to know about other people cannot be identified in separation from their thoughts, imaginings and apprehensions. So, in a great many instances, one's knowledge of one's friend's feelings, wishes and intentions depends on one's knowledge of his thoughts, and these one gathers mainly from his verbal disclosures and communications.

---

[3] For a fuller discussion of this topic see Dilman (1984).

The second reason why one needs to talk to him is the one Malcolm emphasizes, namely that what people tell us about themselves is our most important source of information about them. This is so because a man's feelings and desires may not show in his behaviour, because he can keep these to himself. We are then dependent on his good will — though sometimes his weaknesses and indiscretion lead him to reveal what he would otherwise keep from us. Such cases apart, unless we have his trust he will not talk to us without reserve, he may not find it easy to be open with us.

When a man is divided in himself or in the grip of self-deception, we shall not be able to obtain his whole-hearted trust. The psycho-analyst often finds himself in this sort of situation. Here the growth of the patient's trust in his analyst and his ability to admit to himself what he has been turning away from are two sides of the same coin.

When a man deceives himself about his feelings, the frankest thing he can tell his friend about them will be contrived and the feelings he will express will be false. Here his testimony is not what we should trust, and what he tells us will inform us about his feelings only insofar as it betrays them. Proust was impressed by how often this is the case:

> I, who for so many years had sought for the real life and thought of other people in the direct statements with which they furnished me of their own free will, failing these had come to attach importance, on the contrary, only to the evidence that is not a rational and analytic expression of the truth; the words of themselves did not enlighten me unless they could be interpreted in the same way as a sudden rush of blood to the cheeks of a person who is embarrassed, or a sudden silence. (1952, vol. 5, pt 1, p. 111)

This is something psycho-analysts know very well and observe in their practice.

Thus if a person's testimony is my criterion of what he feels or wishes, it must be given in certain circumstances, uttered in a special tone of voice, and so on. These, at least to some extent, vary from one person to another, and their significance has to be gathered over a certain period of contact with him.

If a person's feelings are what I suspect them to be it doesn't follow that he can admit or express them directly. But if I am right, then, provided that he can come to trust me and has no reason for concealing them, he will be able to avow them. I should deserve his confidence certainly, but equally *he* should be able to put his trust in me. He may have to change in himself if he is to lose his mistrust. But until I have his trust and what I think about him is corroborated by what he tells me, what I think will retain an element of conjecture. For his testimony is my final court of appeal.

A psycho-analyst who finally gets from his patient the testimony which confirms an interpretation with which he has been working may recognize it as genuine straight away. If it is genuine it would have to be backed by changes in the patient's response to the interpretation. Whether or not the analyst recognizes the patient's testimony as genuine straight away, his recognition comes from experience and judgment. There is no general rule or theory which sets out when we can trust someone's self-testimony, in what circumstances what a man says about himself can be taken at face value.

We see that the special weight we attach to a person's words about himself in our appraisal of his feelings and wishes does not imply that we regard him as immune from error or incapable of being deceived. It does not imply that we take these words to disclose to us the results of an infallible introspection.

4   *'Making the Unconscious Conscious'*

I said earlier that even if a person cannot acknowledge his unconscious feelings and desires, it remains true that they are *his*, that he is related to them in a way that no one else can be without being him. This has the consequence that when he finally comes to recognize them he does not do so as a by-stander or an observer. He shows a face to others the outline of which has never presented itself to them this clearly. They *see* what is in question while he *lives* it.

Let us now consider this contrast between a psycho-analyst who comes to see some unconscious attitude or emotion in a patient and the patient himself coming to see

and acknowledge it. In the analyst's case what is in question
is largely an 'aspect change'. As the details of the patient's
past and present circumstances emerge in what he tells the
analyst, as his thoughts and responses find expression in the
course of the analysis, the analyst makes connections which
his patient avoids making and denies, and he comes to see
various features of what the patient discloses in a new light.
They strike him in a new way as he comes to see this in his
own responses to the patient, they take on a new appearance.
This is reminiscent of the way our vision of the expression on
a face may change even when nothing on the face moves or
alters — indeed the face may be one painted by a portrait
artist. Perhaps he comes to see his patient's suffering in a new
light, his apprehension of the latter's character in relation to
this suffering changes. He may in consequence come to see
there something that had not struck him before, perhaps
unconscious feelings of envy and of guilt. It is important to
bear in mind, however, and this is my main point at present,
that this third-person vision itself makes no difference to the
feelings in question. They continue to remain unconscious,
that is hidden from the patient's conscious apprehension,
while the patient himself persists in avoiding any genuine
acknowledgement of them.

It is a different story when he, the patient, finally comes
to recognize them. He does not merely come to see patterns
in his thoughts, feelings and behaviour which he had not
recognized before. He does not merely come to see these in
new constellations. Various elements in the patterns which
constitute these feelings and desires themselves change. Here
Freud talks of what is unconscious becoming conscious. This
is a change in the patient; not merely a change in his understanding. It encompasses his will, so that for instance he stops
going on in certain ways, lets himself go in other ways.

Yet this change in him is not a change in his feelings,
desires and inclinations. If it were, he could not be said
to recognize in them earlier unconscious feelings, we could
not attribute to him a recognition of what he had desired all
along. A psycho-analyst would describe it as a change in the
expression of his feelings and desires. He would say that the
patient was giving them more direct expression now, that he

no longer hid them from himself as well as from other people. In some cases this is a relatively simple change; in others it involves the giving up of a strategy to which the patient was committed. In giving that up the patient may have to work his way out of a complicated posture, one which may constitute an aspect of his character and so of his approach to life as a person.

Freud made it plain that he wanted to talk of the unconscious only where a person actively avoids recognizing his own feelings and desires; that is, where a person is in the grip of self-deception about himself. Hence he talked of what is unconscious as being 'repressed' and he emphasized how much the patient in analysis 'resists' the psycho-analyst's attempts to get him to face what he unconsciously feels, desires and strives after. The instances of self-deception we have here usually combine two features. On the one hand the patient deceives himself by avoiding reflection on his own situation and motives, turning a blind eye to some aspects of his thoughts and behaviour, while exaggerating the influence of others. On the other hand he does so also by putting on certain acts, dramatizing certain events, assuming certain attitudes, taking part in certain activities, avoiding certain situations. In both cases we could speak of appearances being actively arranged and manipulated by him to hide some unwelcome reality. But while in the one case it is solely his apprehension that he tempers with and controls to this end, in the other it is the very things that are the object of his concern that he manipulates. We could say that the changes he effects in order to create an illusion that suits him are both in his thoughts and in what his thoughts are directed to.

Freud's analogy of the student who looks through a microscope and yet 'sees nothing, although it is there and quite visible' (1949a, p. 365) does justice to only one of these features, namely where the deception is an elaborate form of aspect-blindness. But most cases where analysts speak about an unconscious fear or desire involve more than a self-induced aspect-blindness. The thoughts, reveries, actions and activities in which the unconscious fear or desire is active, and so finds expression, are also designed to make it appear that the patient has no such fear or desire — to make it appear that he is indifferent to the object of his desire, not afraid of what spells danger for him. That is, the thoughts and activities in which the fear or desire is active are also strategeies of defence or self-deception. So Freud spoke of them as 'compromise formations'.

It follows that for the patient to gain insight into his unconscious mind requires not only that he should reflect on his life, attitudes, behaviour and thoughts, but also that he should *give up* his strategies of defence, *stop* deceiving himself. One could say that psycho-analytic interpretations are meant to speak not only to the patient's understanding, but also to his will. They bring insight as much by defeating the patient's strategies of defence, or enabling him to dispense with them, as by bringing to his attention features of his character, thoughts and actions, and connecting them in new ways, presenting them under a new aspect. Thus the patient's relation to what, with his analyst's help, he reflects on is different from the analyst's relation to it — or anybody else's. He can assume responsibility for it in a way that the analyst cannot. Ultimately it is up to him whether or not he will stop resisting the analysis and allow what is unconscious to become conscious.[4]

This is where the knowledge and understanding which a patient acquires in analysis differs, and differs profoundly, from any kind of theoretical knowledge and understanding. A person in analysis can certainly pick up new ideas and think of himself in new ways, see his behaviour in a new light. He may pick up a story from a book on psycho-analysis and be convinced that it contains an accurate representation of his own feelings and predicament. What is more, the story may really throw light on what has been under discussion in the analysis. The patient may agree with his analyst's interpretations, and even put forward interpretations himself which anticipate the analyst's interpretations. But if this is all, if it is not backed by the kinds of change I mentioned earlier, the analyst would describe the patient's conviction

---

[4] Ultimately it is up to him whether or not he will change his life, his approach to its problems, his relations with people, his attitude to work, etc.

as 'merely intellectual'. He would say that what he has interpreted so far remain unconscious. The patient is still far from
expressing the feelings and thoughts in question directly,
openly and without subterfuge.

We shall see further down that although the 'enlargement
of consciousness' which we have been discussing here is
essential to acquiring 'knowledge of oneself' it is by no means
the same thing. Self-knowledge goes beyond this transformation of what is unconscious to consciousness. It involves a
change in one's relation to oneself which Freud described in
terms of a change in the ego's relation to the id, the super-
ego, and the outside circumstances of one's life. We can
characterize this as an 'enlargement of the ego, of the sphere
of its autonomy', or as an 'enlargement of the domain of the
will'. I shall return to this topic in chapters 7 and 8.

5

Unconscious Determination: Knowledge and Intention

1 Intention and Consciousness

Freud wanted to speak of people as doing things with certain intentions which they do not acknowledge to themselves — for instance, someone saying something to a friend in order to cause him pain while thinking of himself as saying it for the other person's good. More than this he wished to speak of people as pursuing policies or strategies of which they have no recognition. Yet this *seems* absurd: where a person can be said to exercise his will or agency he *must* know what he is doing, have certain thoughts about his actions and environment. But if his intentions are unconscious he *cannot but* lack such knowledge. And these two conditions seem to exclude each other.

Professor Stuart Hampshire, who has written perceptively both about intention and the unconscious, thinks so: ' "Intention" is the one concept that ought to be preserved free from any taint of the less-than-conscious. Its function, across the whole range of its applications, is to mark that kind of knowledge of what one is doing, and of what one is inclined to do, that is fully conscious and explicit' (1974, p. 125). In *Thought and Action*, where he discusses this question more fully, he argues that there is a 'necessary connection between consciousness and intended action' (1959, p. 94).

The concept of consciousness in question is not the

Cartesian one we criticized in the last chapter. Consciousness, Hampshire argues, is not 'a state of passive awareness'
(1959, p. 94). It is bound up with the human capacity to act
in the full sense of the term, to envisage what one is going to
do, to form projects and intentions: 'Consciousness [is]
inseparable from action, or attempted action, in the sense
that we are always able to answer the question — "What are
you doing now?"' (1959, p. 119). By a man's 'present state
of consciousness' Hampshire does not mean anything like the
private shadows that pass before his inner gaze which at once
lights them up and gives them being — what Iris Murdoch
once characterized as the 'magic lantern' view of consciousness (1953, p. 56). What constitutes a man's present state of
consciousness are his 'present intentions and his beliefs about
his present situation and environment, taken together'
(Hampshire, 1959, p. 101). 'A conscious mind is always
and necessarily envisaging possibilities of action . . . To be a
conscious human being, and therefore a thinking being, is to
have intentions or plans' (p. 119). As for the intentions that
constitute a man's present state of consciousness, Hampshire
is far from regarding them as 'momentary occurrences'
(p. 100) in the way that Descartes would have done.

I agree with and endorse Hampshire's analysis, but I don't
think that it warrants the conclusion which he draws from it,
namely that the notion of an unconscious intention is a contradiction in terms. Certainly to have an intention to do
something is not undergoing an experience or having something going on within one. An intention is not anything like
the sound of a siren, for instance, or a bout of anger (see
Wittgenstein, 1967, sections 81–2). You can pay attention
to the latter, tell when it alters, determine how long it lasts
by means of a stop-watch. It is something that goes on. To
have a intention intermittently, for instance, is not like
having a pain intermittently. An intermittent pain is one that
comes and goes, an intermittent sound is one that is punctua-
ted by intervals of silence, one that is interrupted. In the case
of the intention there is nothing to be interrupted. Rather,
I keep changing my mind, I abandon the intention and then
I return to it. There is nothing continuous that is interrupted;
rather it is I who waver.

No, to have an intention is to envisage doing something in the future. I could be said to have the future action in my thought, though this is not to say that I am thinking of it all the time. I may make up my mind to do something, form an intention, say 'That is settled', and I may not think about it again until the time comes to carry it out. Or I may think of what I am going to do from time to time, that is intermittently. But that doesn't make my intention intermittent. No, I have the future action in my thought in the sense that the declaration of an intention has the form, 'I will do so-and-so'. This, of course, is not a prediction. I do not have inductive grounds for what I say, and I do not wait and see whether it will come true. I proceed to make it come true, I act in conformity with the intention I have announced, or at any rate I try.

If I am to be able to try I must know how to do or bring about certain things, I must have the ability to perform certain actions. If I intend to play chess, for instance, I must be able to do so, know how to play chess, and this obviously is something I have learned. In playing chess I put this knowledge into practice, I utilize or exercise it. It is this knowledge which enables me to have the future action in my thought now in the special way I have it there when I have the intention to do it. Hampshire is right indeed in thinking that there is a 'necessary connection' between my thought or intention and what I intend to do. There is no way of identifying the intention without mentioning the intended action.

An intention may lie in an action, as when we do things with a particular intention, or it may be formed in advance and so precede the action. In the former case it is not something over and above the action, a mental accompaniment of outward movements. The intention with which, for instance, I may dig potatoes into the ground is not something additional to the digging I do. It resides in the way I follow up the digging, the way I go on with what I am doing. This is not something arbitrary. I go on with what I have started in accordance with what I have learned to do. My way of going on belongs with certain farming practices which embody beliefs and expectations about the environment in which I act. What I bring into the first step, the digging, the direction

I bestow on it, comes from my practical knowledge. It is this which enables me to stand in this kind of relation to the future, the relation which constitutes my intention.

There is a lot that a man must have learned before he can have intentions in advance of acting, before he can have intentions which he can abandon without translating them into action. Certainly he has to have learned to do certain things on request and also not to do them. He has to have learned to describe actions and to understand their descriptions. These go together. When he does such an action at will we have seen that the intention lies *in* the action, it has no existence independent of the action. Such an intention acquires a separate existence in the life of an individual only after he has learned, as a child, to consider whether or not to do certain things, when he is able to think about future situations and future developments in his present situation which may call for action now. Where an intention can thus exist apart from the action it anticipates it is still true that unless the agent knows how to perform the action he cannot intend to so. Furthermore to speak of such an intention is still to refer to the pattern the man would realize in performing the action. An unexecuted or half-executed intention makes sense only in relation to executed ones; that is, in relation to the completed action which constitutes its fulfilment. For that is what the agent envisages in forming the intention.

We see that a man who acts intentionally anticipates what he is going to do next, but not in the way an observer does. What he is going to do next is already in his thoughts, it is part of the pattern which constitutes the action he is engaged in or envisages. His knowledge of this pattern, of what constitutes its realization as well as how to realize it, is the practical knowledge which enables him to have in mind what he is going to do next before doing it. Possessing this knowledge and being committed for the future by what he embarks on, or by his intentions, are the two sides of the same coin. To intend to do something is thus to think that one will do it, and doing it intentionally entails knowing what one is doing. What that is cannot be identified independently of the agent's thoughts. That is why he can normally say what he is doing without reflection.

It is this knowledge I have as an agent of my own future actions that Hampshire has in mind when he says that an intention cannot be unconscious. When he speaks of 'consciousness' he means this knowledge and the beliefs presupposed by it, beliefs about one's surroundings. In fact, in ordinary language, 'intentionally' is opposed to 'accidentally' and 'inadvertently', and it means 'with knowledge' (Hampshire, 1959, p. 145). Thus Hampshire speaks of intention as a 'form of knowledge', the peculiar knowledge which an agent has of his own future actions by virtue of his intentions: 'My own conscious intentions are, before all other things, present to me as a form of knowledge and constitute the centre of my consciousness at any particular moment' (p. 133). When he then goes on to list some features of the concept of intention, he writes: 'The subject cannot be ignorant of his intention, although he may make a variety of mistakes in stating it, in putting it into words' (p. 134). My question is: Is this a necessary feature? Does it follow from what Hampshire says about intention as a form of knowledge or consciousness?

Hampshire says: 'If my intentions are . . . unknown to me, then I have no fixed and formed intentions' (1959, p. 103). Indeed, if someone says that he doesn't know what he is going to do or what he intends to do, we take this to mean that he has not yet made up his mind, formed an intention. It isn't that there is something he is going to do which he does not know. If this were the case, he would be surprised by what he does, which means that he was not acting intentionally (see Wittgenstein, 1963, section 628). In that case, what he doesn't know is what he is going to find himself doing. So it is not a case of not knowing what one's intention is or that one has a particular intention — an intention one has formed oneself. But is that really impossible?

A man is considering an invitation the acceptance of which involves his leaving home, and so his family, for a period of time. He is greatly attracted, but he wants to bring his wife's views and wishes into the equation which he is trying to resolve. He starts with an open mind, that is without any formed intentions. But as the dialogue with his wife continues over a certain period, he begins to move towards making up his mind. When his wife points this out to him, he protests. Yet the terms in which he considers the question now give her the impression not merely that he would like to go, but that he has made up his mind to do so and that he is merely seeking her endorsement. Various things he does confirm this impression: he makes inquiries about the journey, clears up his papers, thinks about what he would take with him. But when any of this is brought to his attention, he is always ready with a plausible justification. He feels guilty and uneasy about not thinking enough about his family. Eventually, he chooses the grounds on which 'to make up his mind' to go, those that are the least damaging to his idea of himself as a caring husband and head of the family, doing so a little too ostentatiously.

Can we not say that his mind was already made up before then? Hampshire would say that if he had formed an intention to accept the invitation, he must have *known* he would be going. I do not dispute this, but I claim that a person may know something and still not recognize that he knows it. Certainly when he is able to say to himself, 'I will go', this is a change in him and without this change he could not go in the way he does. For there is a difference between acting as 'an intentional agent in the full sense' and acting with an unconscious intention. Hampshire rightly claims that the change in which a person becomes 'an intentional agent in the full sense' is a change in which he acquires greater freedom in action, one which makes a difference to the responsibility that we attribute to him. I shall return to this question further down.

My point for the moment is this. Certainly the kind of commitment for the future we have in an intention or intentional action involves the agent's knowledge and thoughts in the sense explained. If the agent has an intention then what he intends to do must be in his thoughts and so he must know what he intends to do. The relation between an intention and what would fulfil it is an internal one, so that if someone acts intentionally then he *knows* what he is up to. Still he may know this and not admit it to himself. The husband in the above example does so to keep at bay feelings of guilt provoked by his view of the invitation as a temptation to induldge himself.

It is true that normally the agent's words, when we are satisfied that he is speaking frankly, constitute an important criterion of what he knows and so of what his intentions are. But it is not our only criterion, and in some cases it can be overruled. Normally, when there is a conflict between what the agent says and what certain features of his words and behaviour suggest, once we are satisfied that he is not lying, we go by what he says. There are, however, exceptions to this rule. In some circumstances where there is such a conflict it is not unreasonable to attach little weight to what in other cases weighs heavily. There is no absurdity in this, and I see no contradiction in speaking of a person as knowing something which he won't admit to himself. If so, we can attribute to him the knowledge necessary to his having a particular intention but not a consciousness of the intention.

Hampshire writes: 'Freud has given powerful, almost irresistible, reasons for speaking of unconscious policies and purposes as commonplace facts of human life . . . There is no contradiction or conceptual confusion in the phrase "unconscious purpose". The confusion arises only if intention is separated from consciousness' (1959, pp. 132–3). But I do not see how we could speak of a person as being committed to a policy or as pursuing a strategy without attributing intention to him. Of course Hampshire is right to think that where Freud speaks of 'unconscious intention' a person is not 'an intentional agent in the full sense': 'If being psycho-analysed I am led to acknowledge that I have for years been unconsciously trying to do so-and-so, . . . this bringing into consciousness of a policy that was unconscious makes me thereafter, and for the first time, an intentional agent in this domain of my conduct' (pp. 131–2). The main point is that I can now consider the possibility of giving up the policy, which was previously not open to consideration, and so act differently. But if I could not do so before, this once more raises the question whether, in that case, I could intelligibly speak of an intention: Can one speak of an intention in the absence of choice? Before taking up this question, however, I want to consider further whether we can speak of an intention in the absence of knowledge.

2   *Post-hypnotic Action and the Paradox of Unconscious Intention*

I begin with the case of post-hypnotic action: can it be characterized as intentional? We know that the subject was ordered to do something when in an hypnotic trance. We know that the hypnotist talked to him in a language he understands and also that he is capable of doing what he was asked. We have seen some expression of his willingness to comply. It is true that at the time of the action he has no recollection of the hypnotist's words, and he does not think of himself as obeying anyone. Yet the fact remains that his deeds match the words he heard, understood, and showed a willingness to obey. What is more, if put under hypnosis, he recalls the words and admits he was following instructions. When on this basis we claim that he was obeying an order, we attribute to him the intention to do what he was told. We also attribute to him the knowledge and memory which finds expression in what he does, although it is not accessible to him in the normal way.

So there is a strong analogy between the post-hypnotic subject and a man obeying an order or an actor following stage directions, although there is also a strong disanalogy. If we use words which emphasize both the analogy and the disanalogy this seems to involve us in a contradiction: 'He is obeying an order but he has no idea that he is, and he is unable to do otherwise.' There are two features which seem fatally to go against saying that the subject is obeying an order. The first is that he doesn't know he is obeying an order, he doesn't remember the order. The second is that he is unable to do otherwise. Try as he may he cannot stand on his feet or move them. Or, he feels he must do what he does, he becomes anxious if anyone tries to prevent him.

Can a man be said to be obeying an order when he has no recollection of the order? My wife asks me to bring her the scissors from the bedroom. I go to fetch them. But I am thinking of something else and open the drawer absent-mindedly. I ask myself, 'What did I come here for?' and cannot answer. Would one say that I am looking for the scissors, that I intend to take them to my wife?

Let me alter the example slightly. I do not ask myself what I am doing but I continue to rummage about in the drawer while absorbed in thought. I then sight the scissors, pick them up and take them to my wife. Before I sighted the scissors I did not know what I was doing. Had I been asked I would not have been able to answer. But was I not looking for the scissors all the same? Do not the circumstances give us good reasons for saying that I was?

Besides, what does my lack of knowledge, my failure to remember, consist in? It consists in the fact that I am unable to answer certain questions at the time. This does give us reason for saying that I did not remember what I went to the bedroom for, that I did not know what I was doing. But have we got no reason for saying that I had not forgotten, that I knew what I was doing?

To see that there is, contrast with the following example. Again my wife asks me for the scissors. I say that I shall bring them as soon as I come to the end of the page I am reading. I finish the page, but I continue to read on. After ten minutes she says: 'What about the scissors?' 'Oh,' I say, 'I am sorry, I have completely forgotten. I shall bring them straight away.' What I do not remember here, I still remember in the first example. There, when asked what I am doing, I cannot answer; but I have left my place, I have opened the right drawer, and when I sight the scissors I pick them up.

The use of the words 'I know', 'He knows', 'I remember', 'He remembers' is governed by several criteria which on a given occasion may give us conflicting reasons for wanting to use them. At first we were inclined to say, 'If a man doesn't remember, he cannot be said to obey an order.' We now see that insofar as we have some independent reason for saying that he is obeying an order, we also have some reason for saying that he does remember, that he hasn't forgotten the order. It is true that there is a tie between the concepts of obeying an order, remembering it, and knowing what one is doing. But the use of these concepts is not governed by rigid criteria and is wider than we think at first, going by the most familiar cases. These criteria are complex and it is not necessary for all of them to be satisfied in a particular case for the concept to be applicable.

All the same, what the man himself is able to tell us, or tell himself, is an extremely important criterion for saying that he knows and remembers. Hence when it is not satisfied, however much reason we may have for saying that he knows or remembers, there will be some reason for saying that he doesn't. And this will give us reason for saying that he is not obeying an order. Such a conflict of reasons is inevitable in the cases we are considering. So when asked whether the post-hypnotic subject is obeying an order, the answer is: 'Well, he is and he isn't.' As Wisdom puts it: 'Those situations in which we say of someone that he unconsciously thinks this, imagines that, unconsciously wishes this, feels that, are always ones in which when asked whether he thinks this, imagines that, wishes this, feels that, we are inclined to say "Well he does and he doesn't" ' (1953, p. 277).

Yet there is nothing provisional about this 'He does and he doesn't', 'He is and he isn't'. Nothing further can come to light to modify our answer into 'He seems to be obeying an order, but he isn't really', or 'He is really obeying an order and only pretends not to know anything about it'. For otherwise this would not be a case of someone *unconsciously* obeying an order. Hence the final answer to our question is paradoxical, though there is nothing pernicious in this. For what makes our paradoxical statement true are those respects in which the subject is both like and unlike men whose actions constitute central and familiar instances of obeying an order. If only we could bring these respects vividly before our minds we would see how they exist together and appreciate the sort of picture to which they add up. We would then stop being troubled by 'the incompatibility of the predicates' used to present them.

In Dostoyevsky's story 'The Eternal Husband' we find Velchaninov reflecting on the strange events that came to a climax during the previous night:

'If it is settled that he tried to murder me *accidentally*,' he went on pondering, 'had the idea ever entered his head before, if only as a dream in a vindictive moment?'

He decided that question strangely — that 'Pavel Pavlovitch did want to kill him, but the thought of the murder had never entered his head.' In short: 'Pavel Pavlovitch wanted to kill him but didn't know he wanted to kill him. It's senseless, but that's the truth,' thought Velchaninov.

But more than this — not only had Pavel Pavlovitch wanted to kill him, he had actually sought to do so:

'It was not to get a post and it was not on Bagautov's account he came here, though he did try to get a post here, and did run to see Bagautov and was furious when he died; he thought no more of him than a chip. He came here on my account . . . .' (1950, p. 124)

In other words he had come to a resolution and had sought its fulfilment without knowing it. The story substantiates the truth of Velchaninov's conclusion and so provides an example of what it *means* to seek the fulfilment of an intention without knowing that one is doing so.

If, *in the abstract*, we ask ourselves what this means, it would seem that what we are trying to imagine in the first half of the exercise we are imagining away in the second half. If, instead, we start at the opposite end with the *concrete*, we shall appreciate both why one should wish to speak of an intention in the cases under consideration and also why one should wish to say of the agent that he doesn't know he has such an intention and doesn't recognize the drift and character of his actions. We shall appreciate the way in which what leads us to say the one thing and what leads us to say the other fit together and are different aspects of the same pattern. We shall see that what fulfils the one set of conditions need not exclude what would fulfil the other.

The contrast between these two points of departure is what Freud had in mind when he wrote: 'To most people who have had a philosophical education the idea of anything mental which is not also conscious is so inconceivable that it seems to them absurd and refutable simply by logic' (1949b, p. 10). He said elsewhere that it would be desirable for philosophers to 'first submit to the convincing impressions which may be gained from a first hand study' of the phenomena under consideration (1950, vol. iii). He was urging them to turn their attention to particular cases.

In the particular case of Dostoyevsky's story, Pavel Pavlovitch gets up during the night and tries to cut Velchaninov's throat while the latter is asleep. Considering the events of the previous evening this action seems to come out of the blue. Yet it is not an isolated event, a brain storm. It is an action to which the complicated and bewildering course of events related has led up. What Velchaninov grasps on reflection is the connection between the attempted murder, the time in the past he had spent in the country with Pavel Pavlovitch and his wife, and the subsequent events. But the connection is not a causal one. Briefly, this is what it comes to. In the past Velchaninov had had an affair with Pavel Pavlovitch's wife Natalya. He was in fact the father of their daughter Liza, as Pavel Pavlovitch had found out later. At the time he had wounded Pavel Pavolovitch's pride and had made him jealous. Afterwards the painful events of this period were forgotten by Pavel Pavlovitch, but the feelings of jealousy, hurt pride and humiliation continued to fester in his soul unknown to him. Although the feelings he had nursed had Velchaninov as their object, Dostoyevsky leads us to understand that they had an independent existence in the sense that Velchaninov as a person was incidental to the role he had played in becoming their object. He had simply fitted into a ready-made slot in the triangle he formed in his relationship with Pavel Pavlovitch, as lover of the latter's wife — one which had subsequently been filled by others, including Bagautov. Hence the title of the story: 'The Eternal Husband'. But this is a complication which I shall ignore for our present purposes.

So given the feelings of hurt pride and humiliation, Pavel Pavolvitch sought to take revenge. He also sought to perpetuate something of the old relation — hence the incidents that take place when Pavel Pavlovitch takes Velchaninov to visit the girl to whom he intends to make a proposal of marriage. He was not entirely unaware of his feelings, of the way they oscillated between an abject friendship for Velchaninov and a deep resentment at the latter's response to his abjectness.

But for all this he was unaware of what he was up to. On setting off for Petersburg he had not thought, 'I must go and find Velchaninov'. Yet he seemed to follow Velchaninov until they finally met as if by accident.

The way the meeting took place had a somnambulistic character which Dostoyevsky conveys very well. Compare with the way in *The Idiot* Prince Myshkin and Rogozhin meet at the staircase of the Prince's hotel when Rogozhin pulls a knife and the Prince has an epileptic fit (Dostoyevsky, 1955, Book II, chapter 5). Or the way in *Crime and Punishment* Raskolnikov goes to find Razumikhin: 'Good Lord! I haven't come to Razumikhin after all, have I? I wish I knew whether I've come here of my own accord or by mere chance' (1956, p. 129). Or the way Raskolnikov goes to meet Svidrigaylov in a restaurant: 'I told you of the restaurant myself, and there is nothing miraculous about your coming here . . . Don't you remember?' 'I'm afraid I don't' (p. 478). Pavel Pavlovitch too met Velchaninov in Petersburg in a similar way:

> 'So far as I see, what strikes you most of all is my coming at such an hour and under such peculiar circumstances . . . So that, remembering all the past, and how we parted – it's really strange to me now . . . Though, indeed, I had no intention of calling, and it has only happened by accident . . . '
>
> 'How by accident? Why, I saw you through the window run across the street on tiptoe!'
>
> 'Ah, you saw me! So perhaps you know more about it all than I do! . . . You see, I arrived here three weeks ago on business of my own . . . I am Pavel Pavlovitch . . . you recognised me yourself. I am here to try to get transferred to another province and to a post in another department considerably superior . . . But, all that's neither here nor there . . . The point is . . . that I have been hanging about here for the last three weeks, and I seem to be spinning out my business on purpose – that is, the business of my transfer – and really, if it comes off I do believe I shan't notice that it has come off and shall stay in your Petersburg, feeling as I do now. I hang about as though I had lost sight of my object and, as it were, pleased to have lost sight of it – feeling as I do! . . . ' (1950, pp. 18–19)

He had thought that his object was to find Bagautov and

try to get a transfer. He did not realize that he was seeking to pick up the threads of his old relationship with Velchaninov, to relive the old humiliation and then to avenge himself against the person he had made responsible for it. When I say 'made' responsible I mean that he had encouraged the relationship between his wife and Velchaninov and had derived a certain sustenance from it. And he was doing the same thing now.

If one says that from the start Pavel Pavlovitch was like a spider spinning a complicated web, with a fixed objective, yet oblivious to it, that he engineered much of what happened to him, one would be stressing one aspect of things. One would not be denying that there may have been coincidences, nor that the other people involved played their own part in the events that befell him.

In *Beyond the Pleasure Principle* Freud said that there are cases where the words 'pursuing fate' and 'destiny' cover the facts of men's lives assembled with patience. He then went on to say that much in such men's lives and behaviour which gives the 'impression of a pursuing fate, a demonic trait in their destiny' is 'in a large measure self-imposed' (1948a, p. 22). He wanted to emphasize the extent to which, in Schopenhauer's words, 'every man is the architect of his own fortune' (Schopenhauer, 1951, part VI, p. 63). To emphasize this is *not* to deny what in a different connection may need as much emphasizing, namely how much and how often the direction which men's lives take, and what happens to them, is the result of forces and movements in which they get caught up – and here I do not mean the unconscious, but forces and movements which transcend the individual: wars, political movements, religious conflicts. Each of these have their own part to play in various degrees – the unconscious, coincidences, and forces that transcend the individual.

It is the first of these we are concerned to understand, namely unconscious determination or agency – 'determination' in the sense of 'resolve'. Extreme examples of it are to be found in sleep-walking, automatic writing, post-hypnotic actions and inhibitions. In all these cases the subject cannot help doing what he does. Does this mean that we cannot speak of him as obeying, complying, following?

Certainly the post-hypnotic subject is not doing what he wills. There is no part of him that endorses the action except under the aspect of what he was ordered to do. Let us imagine that he was ordered to stab someone; he picks up a knife and stabs the man in question. Presumably he is fully awake and at the sight of the man he is overcome by an impulse to stab him, on which he acts. If he is acting on impulse does it not follow that his action cannot be characterized as intentional? Not necessarily.

Imagine two different cases. A man is walking on the cliffs and he has a sudden impulse to push his companion off the cliff, and he does so. When questioned he can say nothing more than that he felt like it and had otherwise no reason at all for pushing him – a veritable brainstorm. He did not hate his companion, he had no reason for wanting him dead. He was not responding to anything in his companion, however transitory, which filled him with repugnance. The action comes from a sudden, strong urge which has got detached from an otherwise sane and responsible person's nexus of reasons for doing things. The connections broken make it at least tempting to deny that we have an intentional action here. In another case a man has a good and well paid job. He is bored with it from time to time, but he has never considered giving it up. One day he suddenly has the thought: 'Is it worth slaving for money or security in this way? Wouldn't it be nice to chuck it all in and do something I would really like to do?' He does not pause to consider what it is he would like to do and whether or not he has the means; he goes and hands in his resignation. The thought is sudden and he may have acted irresponsibly, but the action is clearly intentional. He intended to resign his job at the time and he knew what he was doing.

What we describe as 'impulsive action' or 'acting on impulse' has a certain range. It shades and changes into fully intentional action at its upper limit, and it includes irresistible impulse at its lower limit, where a person's action becomes an 'aberration', bearing no relation to the reasons that normally weigh with him. At this extreme we say that he didn't know what he was doing. Where a person has such knowledge, normally he can say 'I am doing so-and-so'. But this is neither necessary nor sufficient. What is crucial is how he goes on with what he is doing at present. What would make us say that the man who pushed his companion off the cliff didn't know what he was doing? Such things as the lightness with which he does so, his immediate response to it. He says, 'I felt like pushing him', but seems oblivious to what is involved in doing this — the consequences for his companion, his family, himself. If he later 'comes to his senses' he may be overwhelmed with remorse at the gravity of his action. He may say, 'He was my friend', 'he was the father of two children', etc. Had he simply forgotten about these things at the time or had he stopped caring about them? There is little difference. The point is that at the time these facts or their significance are blotted out of his consciousness. Were they nevertheless in his thoughts unconciously? I have imagined not. At this extreme 'intention', 'knowledge of what one is doing' and 'having reasons for it' disappear — more or less together.

We see that the fact that a person can be properly described as having acted on impulse does not as such disqualify his action from being characterized as intentional. We see too that a distinction has to be made between a 'brainstorm' and 'unconscious determination'. In the former what a person knows and cares for is temporarily lost to him. In the latter what is not accessbile to him consciously is nevertheless in his thoughts and enters into what he does and how he behaves. The post-hypnotic subject obeys an order which he remembers unconsciously, and he obeys simply because he was ordered. Yet how is this compatible with his acting on impulse? Imagine that it is important for me to get to a place to keep an appointment. I am half way there when I have an accident and suffer a concussion. One possibility is that I am found on the scene of the accident wandering aimlessly all over the place. Another possibility is that I only recall that I have to get to a certain place, not remembering what for. When questioned all I can say is: 'I must get there, but I don't know why.' I will, in all probability, do my utmost to get there. You may try to dissuade me: 'You are in no fit state to go. The roads are treacherous.' But you will not succeed, unless perhaps you can frighten me out of it. You will not succeed because I cannot weigh the reasons you give me against the reasons I have. Not being able to recall them I cannot say to myself: 'I am only going to meet a friend for a meal; it is not a matter of life and death.' Not subject to scrutiny, my reason acquires an absolute character: I only know I must get there, come what may.

The case of the post-hypnotic subject is the same. He only knows he must do whatever it is he was ordered to do, and any reason he may have for not doing it cannot get him to change his mind. His original willingness to comply, his uncritical agreement to carry out the hypnotist's command, has to do with the regressive character of the position into which hypnosis puts him. His sticking to the original intention, after he was woken up, is the result of his mind remaining closed in the way I have suggested, insulated from considerations relating to the time of action and encompassing future consequences. He has no choice; he is prevented from exercising judgment. So we cannot hold him responsible for what he does. Yet if he was ordered to do a degrading thing, this would degrade him. Thus Mario in Thomas Mann's story 'Mario and the Magician'.

An unconscious intention is one which a person cannot give up in the normal way. The agent has no choice but to pursue it. I asked whether in that case we can speak of an intention. I argued that we can. But if we can speak of an intention in the absence of choice, can we speak of autonomy? I have already suggested that we cannot. This means that an unconscious intention is an intention in an attenuated sense. I should now like to explore this a little further.

3   Unconscious Intention and Autonomy

The man executing an unconscious intention is at once agent and victim: he cannot be said to be acting on his own behalf. This is the case with the post-hypnotic subject. But not simply because he is doing what he was told to do. For a man may act in obedience to an order and still act on his own behalf. The question is: in what sort of relation does he stand to the order?

We do sometimes act in obedience to inner voices which

we have not made our own and which are not, therefore, an expression of our will. While we may then certainly be considered responsible for the outcome of what we do, it remains the case that we have not acted as an autonomous agent. For we have not exercised judgment and we have submitted to the demand of these voices. We are responsible, for if anyone suffers as a result, we have no one to blame but ourselves. Yet we were not completely behind what we did, we did not obey the voices in question willingly. So responsibility, in the sense of whether or not one is to blame, does not coincide with autonomy.

The autonomous agent considers himself responsible not in the sense that he may blame himself afterwards, but in the sense that he is willing *now* to pay for the consequences of what he undertakes to do. He has thought about the possible consequences and has weighed them in the light of what he values and cherishes. Having done so he wants to do it and appreciates the risks involved. The action he envisages has his full endorsement. There are two connected points here: (a) that he is wholehearted in what he does; and (b) that he is not the kind of man who will go back on himself. What does it mean to say that he is fully behind his action? We can only answer this question by giving an open-ended list of the way he does not act: He is not acting in order to please or appease anyone. He is not doing so to justify himself before an accuser, whether it be a real person or the inner voice of his conscience. He is not doing so out of fear, acting out of cowardice. He is not doing so rashly, unable to take the time to think. Nor is he doing so at the call of a desire that has made him too eager to act, unable to heed considerations that do normally weigh with him. Of course, an autonomous agent need not reflect each time before he acts. The point is that he is prepared to do so if necessary. He is not rushed into action. His desires are not fragmented or locked in a conflict. The present or the immediate future does not have a greater claim on his attention than any other time. He is in touch with what goes on around him: he is not so absorbed by his present purposes as to forget about other aspects of the matter which normally count for him.

This is not true of a man who executes an unconscious

intention or pursues an unconscious policy. He is so taken up by his present purposes that there isn't enough of him left to mind the considerations that do weigh with him. Yet he differs from a 'single-minded' person in that his single-mindedness does not have his full consent. What he is seeking is unwelcome to the rest of him or it can only be achieved at a price which he finds unacceptable. That is why it has been segregated from the rest of his concerns and interests and carried out without their backing.

Consider Pavel Pavlovitch again. He goes to Petersburg to kill Velchaninov though he doesn't know this. How does this differ from Raskolnikov going to the house of the money-lender, intending to kill her? Granting that in both cases there is the intention to kill someone, what difference does the subject's lack of awareness make to what he does? How is this difference mirrored in our respective reactions? If Pavel Pavlovitch knew what the story reveals about him, he could not have carried on with his relationship to Velchaninov in Petersburg in the way he does. If he had, this would have been a pretence and he would have been a different person — a more evil and sinister character altogether. In fact he is rather a pathetic character: rushing about frantically, but passive and long suffering.

Raskolnikov too is a passive character, though his passivity is buried (see Snodgrass, 1960), but he is not pathetic. The violence that is in him is more at his disposal, and in the execution of the murder he differs from Pavel Pavlovitch. He plans it down to the minutest detail; he is determined not to leave anything to chance. He chooses the time, the manner of its execution, and the weapon. The one thing that he doesn't choose and which throws him off is the appearance of the pawnbroker's meek sister Lizavetta Ivanovna in the scene of the murder. Raskolnikov had mobilized himself into action by representing the pawnbroker to himself as wholly evil and utterly despicable. In introducing Lizavetta into the scene Dostoyevsky seems to be telling Raskolnikov that evil and good come mixed together and that he cannot destroy the one without injuring the other. One could say that the pawnbroker Alyona Ivanovna, represented by Raskolnikov as a blood-sucking louse, is an object of phantasy. In translating the violence inspired by it into action, however, Raskolnikov acts on the real world. The fact that Lizavetta is one of the casualties of his action is a constant reminder to him of the difference between his dreams and the real world.

Given this serious qualification Raskolnikov is nevertheless active in planning and executing the murder. There is, it is true, much in him that resists it and which he has to control in order to put his intention into action; and afterwards, in the course of the narrative his hold on it gradually weakens and finally crumbles. Dostoyevsky represents this as a new dawn for Raskolnikov; but with this we are not now concerned. The point of concern for us is that in seeking to execute a conscious intention one has to reckon with reality, and one may have to gather oneself, willingly give up something else or put it aside. Of course there may be unforseen consequences which may take one by surprise. Also after the execution the action may look different to the agent from the way it did at the stage of planning. In some cases this is a failure of imagination, in others it is an expression of the way the action changes the agent. Raskolnikov is changed by what he does to the point of finally repudiating it and taking on responsibility for what he has done. This is the sense of responsibility which earlier I equated with autonomy.

Unlike Raskolnikov, Pavel Pavlovitch does not plan the murder he unconsciously intends to carry out. To be able to plan, to take precautions, in the way that Raskolnikov does, his intention has to be fully conscious. He knows where to find Velchaninov, of course, and pursues him as in a dream. Having found him he knows how to entangle him in a relationship which repeats an earlier pattern. But there is no planning beyond this degree of unconscious manipulation. Much is left to the mercy of chance events. Pavel Pavlovitch does not poise himself for the action in advance, he does not gather himself in the way that Raskolnikov does. When he picks up the threads of the old relationship with Velchaninov he is not being hypocritical. On the fatal night, before he takes Velchaninov's razor and tries to cut his throat, he is beside himself trying to relieve Vechaninov's pain 'as though it were a question of saving his own son'. This is not something he puts on.

Reflecting on the incident immediately afterwards Velchaninov comes to one distinct conclusion: 'That Pavel Pavlovitch certainly had meant to cut his throat, but that perhaps only a quarter of an hour before he had not known that he would do it. The razorcase had perhaps merely caught his eye the evening before, and, without arousing any thought of it at the time, had remained in his memory' (Dostoyevsky, 1950, p. 121).

What took place in Velchaninov's room that night was no accident. Nor was it the case that Pavel Pavlovitch formed the intention to murder his friend on the spur of the moment. Dostoyevsky suggests too much arrangement for that to be a likely story. Yet if Pavel Pavlovitch had succeeded in killing Velchaninov this could not have been an instance of what the law describes as a 'premeditated murder' in the way that Raskolnikov's murder of the pawnbroker, but not of her sister, was.

Pavel Pavlovitch becomes conscious of his intention to kill Velchaninov in his attempt to kill him. He would have to cast his mind back, however, and reflect on the course of events that led up to it before he could shoulder responsibility for it. We find him unwilling to do this. In the event he gives up the intention and leaves Petersburg. But he sticks to his character. Two years later Velchaninov finds him married to a young and attractive provincial lady, as abject as before in his relationship with her, and she as responsive to the attentions of a third party. To give up the intention to murder Velchaninov, in the role of the third party who had wronged him, he had to wake up to having it. But to extricate himself from the pattern which Dostoyevsky marks by calling him 'the eternal husband' he has to become conscious of a great deal more.

In the last chapter we saw that when an unconscious feeling becomes conscious more is involved than a person grasping what the indirect expression of this feeling in his behaviour and actions amounts to. The person loses the fear of owning the feeling, finds the courage to give it more direct expression, and he grasps the identity between what he previously tried to hide and what he now expresses openly. He stops deceiving himself and loses a fear; but he still has the problem of what to do about the way he feels. Analysis helps him to find his own solution. It does so by enabling him to bring more of himself to bear on his problems and by pointing to him where he deceives himself in the solutions he seeks.

In the present chapter we saw that similarly when an unconscious intention becomes conscious more is involved than a change in the person's understanding of what he is seeking. He finds, for the first time, the opportunity to assess critically his reasons for wanting to pursue the course of action intended and either to pursue it and take responsibility for it or to give it up. With an unconscious intention a person lacks this opportunity, and he is therefore not an agent in the full sense: he is both agent and victim at the same time. Similarly, in many of the cases where a patient in analysis complains of being in a rut or trapped in a pattern of behaviour which he wishes to shake off, it turns out that he is at once the gaoler and the gaoled. That is why analysis is a form of treatment that requires and cannot advance without the patient's active participation.

6

Repression and Self-deception

1 Repression: a Curtailment of Autonomy

Psycho-analytic interpretations, I said earlier, are meant to speak to the patient's will as much as to his understanding (see p. 61 above). They are aimed at undoing repression, and repression is 'the struggle against acceptance of a painful part of reality' (Freud, 1950, vol. i, p. 297). It is the person himself who is engaged in this struggle, he defends himself actively. He is 'keeping something out of consciousness', 'rejecting' it (vol. iv, p. 86).

In his *Introductory Lectures* Freud contrasts this with the conscious giving up of a desire or intention (1949a, p. 248). The giving up of a desire often takes self-mastery. Whereas repression is at the other end of the pole. As we shall see, where a person consciously restrains himself or gives up a desire, the ego (Freud would say) acts on its own behalf; whereas in repressing it the ego acts at the behest of the super-ego (1949b, p. 75). Besides, a repressed desire is not a desire that one has given up. One secretly holds on to it while forbidding oneself to seek its satisfaction. One also avoids recognizing that one has such a desire. One may attempt to convince oneself that one has no such desire. So there are two components to repression, though in practice these merge together and serve each other's purpose: unconscious self-denial and self-deception — denial of indulgence and expression, and denial of recognition.

Compare with the repression of a people or section of the community by a dictatorial regime. (a) The regime does not allow the people to do what they want. Certain pursuits are declared illegal and are not permitted. (b) The regime does not allow the people to express certain opinions and aspirations, to voice their grievances, to criticize its conduct. (c) By means of propaganda and rhetoric it may attempt to mould people's opinions to its own liking and advantage. If, in consequence, the people do not give it much trouble, that is because they are either cowed or deceived, or both. If they are completely deceived they will toe the line and support the regime willingly. But insofar as they are merely cowed, they will not have given up their aspirations; the regime will not have their consent. Not only will they continue to be critical of it, though privately, but they will have additional ground for dissatisfaction and resentment. This resentment, if it is not allowed expression, will fester into bitterness and erupt into violence. That is, repression breeds violence, because it shows no consideration towards the people it controls and is opposed to them, and because it stifles their lives. Repressive regimes which realize this danger sometimes provide 'safety valves' to avert the danger of becoming the object of this pent up violence. They encourage people to find scape-goats and even engage in war to give people an opportunity to let out their anger. Here we have some analogy to Freud's conception of symptoms as 'substitute formations' which permit 'the return of the repressed' in a manner that does not endanger 'the security of the ego'.

In the kind of repression which Freud has in mind there is a similar opposition and lack of consent, but it is between two different aspects of the same person. This raises philosophical questions about how the opposition and the unwillingness is to be understood. How and to what extent do the categories in terms of which we think of what goes on in the relations between a tyrannical regime and its people have to be modified in understanding the Freudian concept of repression? Secondly, the aim of repression includes ensuring that one does not recognize having the thought, emotion or longing in question. Obviously this can only be ensured if one can also ensure, simultaneously, that one remains unaware of one's role in bringing it about. And the philosophical question is: How is this possible? How is the notion of a man deceiving himself to be understood?

I spoke earlier of two components of repression; these are in fact two aspects of the same thing. For if one is to remain unaware of an emotion or desire one will have to check giving way to the emotion, to restrain oneself from seeking to satisfy the desire — at least openly and without disguise. Conversely, if one is to be able to restrain oneself in this way, it will help if one can deceive oneself about the object of the emotion or desire, represent it to oneself as less provocative or less desirable than one finds it in reality. So under whichever aspect one considers the matter, one is dealing with a certain kind of self-division, and there are problems about how the quasi-autonomy of the divided parts is to be understood. Can we say, for instance, that under one of these aspects a person knows something which he doesn't know under the other aspect? Can we say that under one of these aspects he is active, while under another he is a passive recipient of the consequences of this activity — a victim of his own projects?

Earlier I contrasted voluntary self-restraint and repression. In conscious, voluntary self-restraint or self-denial there is no division of will. Thus a person may forgo doing what attracts him because he believes it to be wrong. For instance he sees the money offered him under the aspect of a bribe. It is different where he forgoes it under threat, or because he is afraid that others will frown on him. In the first case though the money may attract him, he is still doing what he himself wants in not accepting it. He is at one with his refusal. What gives his will the unity that it has are the moral beliefs that he has made his own.

Cases of repression are those in which a person has not been able to achieve such unity of will. What is more, resorting to repression impedes its achievement. For the motive behind repression is either fear or the safeguarding of a sectional interest of the self. I mean, for instance, a need which has not been accepted by the rest of the self, endorsed, or made one's own. So if one seeks to satisfy it one will not be fully behind the actions one takes in its pursuit. Thus Freud points out that people often resort to repression as a means to coming to terms with a painful conflict, and he observes that it ensures that the conflict remains unresolved. For in-

stance, a person may find his sensuality unacceptable, think
of himself as demeaned by it, and so try to deny it altogether.
In time this may transform him into someone dry, self-
righteous and pompous, speaking a lot about decency but with
little capacity for warmth and generosity. Such a person will
not have resolved his conflict. He will only have stopped
being aware of it since he will have gagged his sensuality. He
will have done so in part by making the voice in him that
speaks of decency increasingly more clamorous and harsher.
As we listen to him we shall feel that this voice is not really
his, that the conviction which it is meant to express is not
wholly genuine. It is whipped up, devoid of the kind of
repose that belongs to genuine conviction. This is the voice
of repression, and in it we can discern the same intolerance
towards other people as he shows towards himself. It serves
a 'sectional interest': Freud characterizes it as the voice of
the super-ego.

As for the fate of the repressed, Freud points out that it
continues to exist and to press for expression and recognition.
It has only been 'abolished from consciousness'. Therefore
the person has to continue to maintain the repression: 'Repression is not to be regarded as something which takes
place once for all ... It demands a constant expenditure
of energy, and if this were discontinued the success of the
repression would be jeopardised' (1950, vol. iv, p. 89).
Depending on how successful it is, the repressed may find
some indirect form of expression, or it may return under a
disguise in the form of 'symptom formation'. So Freud
says that 'repression leaves *symptoms* in its train' (p. 93).

Repression, then, is something which the person engages
in or does. Freud attributes it to the agency of the ego. It
involves denying expression to a thought or emotion which
the person finds unacceptable. This is the part of the person
in which he has taken sides with figures from the past who
have been concerned in disciplining him. Freud refers to it
as the super-ego. There are many devices which a person
may resort to in maintaining repression. He may avoid
situations which provoke the unwelcome emotion or turn
his thoughts away from subjects which threaten to stir it
up. He may develop contrary emotions and attitudes, culti-

vate interests that keep him on safe ground. But in what he does he has ulterior motives and he is not fully behind the steps that he takes. That is why I said that the denial we have here is not genuine or authentic. Furthermore, because it is a denial that comes from fear it is intolerant. Thus in repression a person takes up an attitude towards aspects of himself which is unaccepting. It is an attitude that perpetuates self-division.

Turning away from such an attitude, as this may come about in the course of psycho-analytic therapy, does not necessarily mean giving in to what one has so far repressed. (I shall say more about this in chapter 11 below.) Accepting and giving in are two different things. Thus a parent can accept a child, with all his faults, without spoiling him. Generally indulgence is a sign of either weakness or lack of standards. But, as we shall see, having a strong super-ego is not the same thing as having high standards.

2   Self-deception and Inauthenticity

In *L'Être et le Néant* Sartre develops an account of self-deception, which he calls 'bad faith', and he criticizes Freud for evading the difficulty at the heart of this concept by splitting 'the psychic whole in two'. In this way, he argues, Freud is able to represent self-deception as the deception of one person, or sub-person, by another. Whereas in self-deception a person is at once both deceiver and deceived: 'Bad faith implies the unity of a *single* consciousness.' Hence the paradox of self-deception. Quite rightly, Sartre stresses that the deception we have in bad faith is *willed* by the self; it is not something that is simply suffered. Bad faith 'is not a *state* . . . There must be an original intention and a project of bad faith.' But how can a person keep from himself what he must know in his capacity as deceiver? Besides, if the deceiver intends to deceive himself, he must also be deceived about his intention. Yet is not a recognition of what he is trying to avoid recognizing implicit in such an intention? (I have discussed this question in chapter 5 above.)

Sartre claims that Freud had 'recourse to the unconscious'

in order to 'escape from these difficulties'. By means of 'the hypothesis of a censor' he tried to 're-establish the duality of the deceiver and the deceived'. The difficulties which Sartre raises are genuine philosophical difficulties, and it is true that to resort to the concept of the unconscious, to speak of a censor in the mind, would not resolve these difficulties, but only postpone confronting them. On the other hand, this is not the reason why Freud talked in the way he does. Sartre is right, as I agreed, that we cannot represent repression as 'the impact of blind forces'. But, I have argued, Freud would have agreed. Sartre takes Freud's language too much at face value.

There are, of course, other forms of self-deception which Sartre does not recognize, forms of self-deception which do not raise the difficulties which Sartre discusses, but other ones which he does not discuss (see Dilman and Phillips, 1971). These are not relevant to our present discussion, so I shall pass them by without mention. Cases where a person deceives himself about his feelings and desires which he does not allow direct expression in his behaviour are different and nearer to the examples Sartre had in mind. But here too there are differences worth noting. Thus think first of the case of a man who tries to keep at bay an unwelcome recognition about himself, say his egotistical character, which would disturb his equinimity. It need not be the case, even here, that he knows or suspects 'underneath' that he is egotistical. It is sufficient that he should find it unwelcome to think of himself in this way, so that when anything gives him a reason to do so he evades the inference, finds or invents himself a reason ('rationalization') for not drawing such a conclusion. What is necessary is that he should be capable of drawing such a conclusion – which he in fact does in the case of other people. By evading certain conclusions which other people may find irresistible he is able to preserve the illusion of being a generous person who cares for other people. Obviously it matters to him to be able to think of himself this way; otherwise he could not go on in the way he does with impunity. He thus defends an illusion about himself against anything that threatens it. But it does not follow that he knows it to be an illusion. His object is to avoid coming to have such knowledge, *not* to avoid becoming conscious of the knowledge he already has.

Here the deception is *willed* in that it is he who preserves or safeguards the illusion, keeps at bay or disarms whatever threatens it. However, it is possible for him to have this same illusion about himself naively so that it does not amount to self-deception. In other words, where he is self-deceived, what makes him the agent of the deception is distinct from what makes him its victim. The kind of division we have in this case is a straightforward conflict which should not present any difficulty for Sartre. On the one hand our man is inclined to be selfish, while on the other hand he finds recognition of this unwelcome and so is disinclined to admit it to himself. Surely he can go along with the latter inclination without defeating the former one.

There is, however, a difference between wishing to *be* different from the way one is and wishing to *think* one is different, even though the line between the two cases is not a sharp one. In the case of our egotistical man, if it is the case that he wishes he *were* different, this would mean that he is dissatisfied with himself. It is not so much his 'self-image' that he is concerned with as the way he *is*. This would mean that he has some recognition of the character of his actions with regard to other people and is troubled by it. This, in turn, would presuppose some feeling in him for other people. In that case there are three different things he could do, the attractiveness of these alternatives depending on his character and on how deep his feelings for other people go. (a) The guilt and repentence he feels for some of the things he has done or evaded doing may bring him out of himself; he may begin to put himself out for people in a way he has not done before. (b) He may opt for some sort of compromise to be able to carry on as before, try to appease his conscience to relieve himself of the burden of guilt. (c) He may try to stick to his old ways and attempt to persuade himself that what he feels about himself is illusory.

With this last case of self-deception we come to the difficulties raised by the aspect of Freud's concept of repression under consideration. For indeed part of what is involved here could be described as the repression of feelings of guilt. Let us remember that a feeling of guilt itself involves a judgment or apprehension, even if the judgment may be confused or the apprehension distorted. If a person feels guilty about the way he behaves towards other people he must see his behaviour in a certain light and feel unhappy with what he sees. This means that certain things matter to him, that he has certain standards. To deceive oneself about one's feelings of guilt, (a) one would have to come to believe that things are not as one feels them to be, at least that they are not as bad, and (b) one would have to concoct a form of elation ('manic defence') which carries one out of the orbit of the sense of unworthiness which dampens one's expansiveness. In practice these two targets merge and intermingle with each other.

To begin with one's apprehension of one's egoism. Things are not normally very clear cut here and there are many different plausible voices and arguments which one can adopt or side with. One's very wish to avoid seeing oneself in a painful light will add authority to the voices one is pleased to hear. The man in our example may mix with people whose ways of thinking, interests and tastes he finds supportive, and he may avoid those whose critical approach constitutes a threat to his purposes. He may, further, mistake and even avoid reflecting on the character of what attracts him in the first kind of people, indulgent, undemanding and light-hearted, and what repels him in the second group of people whom he describes in uncomplimentary and unfair terms. These very terms, which may have the backing of the group with which he identifies himself, may serve to fend off scrutiny. He may, further, indulge in easy gestures of generosity, associate with action groups which give him a sense of purpose and a feeling of doing something. The headiness of it all may make it difficult for him to see how little of himself he gives to others. The very badges he displays are part of this elaborate cover-up, part of this living the life of a borrowed self to avoid recognizing the selfishness and poverty of his own life.

As for the 'manic defence', he may give himself to activities which involve 'fun and gaiety', cultivate light-hearted friendships which thrive on mutual back-patting, avoid situations which may bring to his attention the more serious side of things.

There is obviously much here that he concocts, arranges, allows himself to be caught up in, avails himself of and uses, avoids or turns away from. Hence his agency. All this is designed to influence and manipulate his view of himself, represent certain doubts he has as groundless, certain thoughts he has as illusory. He even uses other people to manipulate his view of himself, to contradict the judgment implicit in the guilt he feels. Yet given the independent life of these activities, patterns of behaviour, relationships, it is not too difficult for him not to see his ulterior motives, to misapprehend the character of his involvement in them.

The part he plays in creating the favourable view of himself which takes him in is an aspect of the way he lives and acts. So long as he continues with it, this means that he needs convincing and, therefore, that he is not wholly convinced. It means that if he were to stop, to give up the subterfuge, his doubts would reassert themselves, feelings of guilt would disturb his peace. His peace of mind is precarious, it has to be constantly bolstered up. This means that while he succeeds in convincing himself that he has no grounds for feeling guilty, he nevertheless continues to think of himself as ungiving and uncaring, and to feel bothered and guilty about it. He continues to deceive himself just because there is a part of him that knows otherwise and is not duped. Insofar as he succeeds in deceiving himself he will not feel guilty; but insofar as he needs to deceive himself it will remain the case that he continues to feel guilty. It is precisely this that makes makes Freud speak of the feelings of guilt here as unconscious.

'He is convinced that all is well and that there is no cause to feel guilty.' 'He doubts that all is well and continues to feel guilty.' In the abstract these words contradict each other. Yet if we consider the reasons which in our particular example support what we say by means of the one set of words and those which support what we say by means of the other set we shall appreciate that they do not exclude each other. On the contrary, those features of our example which give us reason to say the one thing and those which give us reason to say the other knit together *one* of the familiar faces of self-deception – the very one which Sartre had in mind. These are, indeed, the very features which justify the claim that the man in our example feels guilty unconsciously, or in his unconscious mind. But unless we can appreciate this, reference to unconscious guilt or knowledge will not take us further than where we were when we thought that the notion of self-deception involves a contradiction. For, to alter very slightly Wisdom's words I quoted earlier (see p. 72 above). 'Those situations in which we say of someone that he unconsciously feels guilty, or knows that he behaves selfishly, are always ones in which when asked whether he feels this or knows that, we are inclined to say, "Well he does and he doesn't".' If, on the other hand, we do appreciate it, we shall not need the second description to resolve our difficulty.

As for Sartre's claim that 'bad faith implies in essence the unity of a single consciousness', what it comes to is that in self-deception the deceiver and the deceived are the same person. However, this does not imply, as Sartre puts it, 'the unitary structure of a single project'. For, as we have seen, in the kind of example we have considered, the person *is* divided in his will. For insofar as he feels guilty he does want to act differently from the way he does – to consider other people, to make amends for his selfishness and insensitive treatment of them. Yet his attempt to deceive himself is an expression of his will to continue to behave as before, selfishly, without paying the cost for it.

Thus for a person to become conscious of what is unconscious in him, for him to acknowledge the truth of what he deceives himself about, he must not only reflect on himself, but also stop running away, give up his defences. In this way he will not only shed a burden that weighs him down, but he will become a more genuine person. Because the kind of deception we have considered is more than a self-induced aspect-blindness, but involves an active participation in certain forms of behaviour and the adoption of certain postures, deceiving oneself involves becoming *false*. For what the deceived person engages in is subservient to what he finds frightening, painful, damaging to his self-esteem, or a threat to his ability to continue with modes of behaviour he clings to though they do not have his full consent. Hence turning away from deception is turning towards a more authentic existence.

A person who does so will normally find in himself a greater capacity to give and take, to enjoy life and take an interest in what it offers, as well as a greater openness to pain and grief. When he stops protecting himself he will become more alive. Here Freud spoke of the energy used in repression becoming available to the person for positive expansion: 'We may imagine that what is repressed exercises a continuous straining in the direction of consciousness, so that the balance has to be kept by means of a steady counter-pressure. A constant expenditure of energy, therefore, is entailed in maintaining a repression, and economically its abrogation denotes a saving' (1950, vol. iv, pp. 89—90). What is in question is not anything like the energy in a mechanical system, but the 'wasting of oneself' on what one has little interest in except for purposes of defence. The case of someone who is so intent on keeping up appearances that he makes himself unavailable to any genuine relationship offers some analogy to what Freud had in mind. Secondly, the emotions which a person 'locks in' through the kind of restraint involved in repression leaves him less able to make contact with people, poorer in initiative and standing-power where his beliefs are concerned, and less capable of giving himself to interests that would enrich him.

I spoke of the division of will that is inevitably involved in repression. Further consideration of the nature of this division takes us straight into the question raised by Freud's conception of the divisions of the personality. These questions are the topic of the following chapter.

7

Divisions of the Personality

1 Divisions of What? Some Questions

It was post-hypnotic behaviour and recollection under hypnosis that first opened Freud's mind to the possibility that we may not know what is in our own minds and that what is there, unknown to us, may enter into and play a decisive role in what we do and what we suffer. While he insisted that a person is related to his own unconscious mind differently from the way others are related to it, that what is in question is his own mind, he did not forget that repression separates him from his unconscious ideas, feelings and desires in a way in which he is not separated from his conscious mind. At first Freud's interest centred on what a person repudiates in himself, turns away from, and on how nevertheless it plays a determining role in his behaviour. Later he turned his attention to the person's role in this form of repudiation in which he appears as set against himself.

Here we have already, from the beginning, what Freud later characterized as the division between the ego and the id. The ego is what does the repudiation, the turning away, and the id is what is repudiated, checked, denied expression. There are already difficulties here to which I shall return presently. What I want to point out, before I do so, is Freud's realization that this distinction between the ego and the id does not coincide with and cuts across his distinction between the conscious and the unconscious. For, as we have seen, the person is unaware of himself in his active role of repudiating the way he may be attracted to certain prospects and the way he actually visualizes them. This recognition opened Freud's mind to the possibility that the ego may itself be unconscious, so that it does not coincide with 'consciousness' (including what Freud called 'the preconscious').

I said something about Freud's justification for regarding the unconscious as something more than what is designated by a collective noun. Here Freud talked of the unconscious as a 'system' and of the 'systematic sense' of the term 'the unconscious'. He carried this idea over to his concepts of the ego and the super-ego and talked of these as 'mental structures' or 'agencies', as constellations within the mind or 'parts' of the person or personality. He thought of the id as an unstructured part of the personality. But there are difficulties here: how are we to understand the notion of a part in this connection? We could say, for instance, of someone who denies all responsibility for something that has happened, that 'in part of himself' he feels he is to blame and blames himself, or that there is 'a part of him' which knows that he shares some of the responsibility. Again we have heard people speak of conflicts in themselves in terms of certain abstractions: 'My reason tells me one thing and my heart tells me something different.' In his concepts of the ego, the super-ego and the id Freud takes this way of talking further. We want to ask: How does it further our understanding of the questions that preoccupied him ?

When one talks of a conflict between, say, the head and the heart, between duty and inclination, one is talking of the conflict in which a person finds himself. It is *he* who has to consider the conflicting voices, weigh the conflicting reasons, with a view to resolving the conflict, arriving at a decision. But is what Freud calls 'the ego' a part of the personality on a par with the others? Freud is in two minds. He does see that all conflicts involve the ego, involve it as *subject*: it is the ego that is pulled in different directions, that has to respond to the conflicting demands made on it. Yet he resists equating the ego with the person because he wishes to say that there are other sides to the person. For if the id and the super-ego are parts of the person, they are not parts of the ego. And this pushes him to characterize the ego as a structure of the mind, a system within the mind, a part of the personality, a

mental agency with certain functions. As far as I can see this
conflict belongs to his way of speaking and cannot be resolved
without modifying that way of speaking.

Freud wanted to emphasize that there is more to a person
than his conscious personality, that there are aspects of him
that he does not recognize. His activities and intentions have
dimensions of which he is not aware — the unconscious ego.
If he were aware of them he would naturally speak of them
in the first person: 'I am inclined to do so-and-so', 'I won't
do such-and-such'. Then he has desires, emotions and memories which he won't admit to although they are still *his*.
Insofar as he becomes aware of their influence, this seems to
him to have its source outside him; and indeed what is in
question is external to his will. Thus in his *New Introductory
Lectures* Freud characterizes 'the repressed' as 'a foreign
territory to the ego' (1933, p. 82). The impulses a man
becomes subject to, the times when he cannot stop himself
doing what he does, or manage doing what he wants and
ought to be able to do: here Freud finds an aspect of the
person independent of his will. From the perspective of his
will, conscious and unconscious, what issues from it is something which the ego suffers. Freud refers to it as the 'id' and
says that the 'impersonal pronoun seems particularly suited
to express the essential character of this province of the mind'
(p. 102)

The third aspect of what more there is to the person than
his 'conscious ego' Freud identifies as his 'super-ego'. While
he does not completely equate this with what we normally
mean by 'conscience', he thinks of 'conscience' as an aspect
of the super-ego. My difficulty is that while I can understand
contrasting a man's conscience, his sense of duty for instance,
with his sensual desires, in the sense that these may come
into conflict in particular circumstances, I do not see any
easy justification for contrasting his conscience with his ego
in the sense of himself. I am, therefore, more inclined to think
of the super-ego as an extension of the ego, although I can
see that this would not satisfy Freud (see section 4 below).

The modification I have suggested to Freud's tripartite
division of the personality is this. The known and familiar
ego becomes the *centre* from which a person acts, takes

decisions, resolves his conflicts, reasons and makes judgments. The unconscious ego and the super-ego, conscious and unconscious, become extensions of this centre. The id remains that dimension of the person which, on the whole, Freud regards as representing his membership of the species as a biological unit. It is characterized by the kind of mentality on which I have commented in chapter 3. When contrasting it with the ego Freud refers to it as 'the repressed', but it is not clear whether he regards it as coextensive with the repressed. In *The Ego and the Id* he says that 'the ego is that part of the id which has been modified by the direct influence of the external world' (1949b, p. 29). I take it that he is referring to the development of self-awareness. He repeats this in *An Outline of Psycho-Analysis*: 'Originally . . . everything was id; the ego was developed out of the id by the continual influence of the external world. In the course of this slow development certain material in the id was transformed . . . and taken into the ego. Other material remained unaltered in the id, as its hardly accessible nucleus' (1949c, pp. 23–4). So he makes a distinction between 'two categories of material in the id', namely 'what was originally present and what was acquired during the development of the ego' (p. 24). The same distinction is made in his earlier paper on 'The Unconscious' between the 'inherited mental formations' which 'constitute the nucleus of the unconscious', 'the primary unconscious', and later additions of 'all that is discarded as useless during childhood development' (1950, vol. iv, p. 127). Is it only the latter that is to be characterized as 'repressed'? One could argue that what has never reached consciousness and subsequently been prevented by the ego from doing so can also be subsumed under the category of the repressed. But when Freud speaks of the way the ego has developed out of the id what does he mean by 'the transformation of certain material in the id'?

I take it that what is in question is the way certain 'primitive reactions' (Wittgenstein), arising out of various common impulses, form the basis of certain 'language-games' and are 'extended' in these language-games: 'Our language-game is an extension of primitive behaviour' (Wittgenstein, 1967, section 545). Wittgenstein is here thinking of our response to people in pain; but this is only a particular example and what he says has wider application. He describes the response or reaction on which the language-game is based as 'natural' and 'instinctive'. Any such language-game belongs to a natural language, such as English or German, and is embedded in a whole way of living or 'culture' (1969a, p. 134). It is in learning to speak this language and assimilating the culture that the individual is transformed; and this includes what he becomes capable of cognizing and experiencing — cognizing in himself and elsewhere. Insofar as we regard some of the things he becomes capable of feeling in adulthood as continuous with the feelings that find expression in these primitive, instinctive reactions, we could speak of the original feelings (belonging to the id, as Freud would say) as *transformed* when they become the object of the person's awareness. In *The Ego and the Id* Freud asks: 'How does a thing become conscious?' He answers: 'By coming into connection with the verbal images that correspond to it' (1949b, p. 21). The question refers to the emergence of self-consciousness in the development of the individual. He connects this with the acquiring of language in the way I suggested.

    What is in question here, what I called 'the emergence of self-consciousness', should not be confused with what I discussed earlier under the sub-heading of 'making the unconscious conscious' (see chapter 4, section 4, above). And so Freud's question above should be distinguished from the question he asks in his paper on 'The Unconscious': 'When a mental act is transferred from the system Ucs into the system Cs (or Pcs), are we to suppose that this transposition involves a fresh registration . . . or are we rather to believe that the transformation consists in a change in the state of the idea . . . ?' (1950, vol. iv, pp. 106—7). For here the person, a patient in analysis, has already got the concept of what he avoids recognizing in himself and the capacity to recognize it. Whereas in the question Freud raises in *The Ego and the Id* he is concerned with the emergence of this capacity in the development of self-awareness. And there are difficulties here, not insuperable, concerning the identity between the early desire, phantasy or emotion attributed to the infant, though he was not capable of being conscious of it, and the later desire or emotion of which he is conscious or becomes conscious in analysis. There is, too, the prior difficulty concerning the intelligibility of attributing these, in however primitive a form, to a creature, namely the infant, who lacks speech and self-awareness.

2   Freud's Conception of the Id

So Freud thinks of the id as that in the infant out of which the ego or individual self develops, as well as that in the adult which survives this development. This concept is continuous with his earlier concept of the unconscious to which in his paper 'The Unconscious' (first published in 1915) he attributes a special mentality in sharp contrast with the adult person's conscious mentality. We have seen that he regarded the unconscious both as what is repressed and also as what predates consciousness and self-awareness in the development of the individual. It is this second aspect of the unconscious that he takes up in the concept of the id.

As Earnest Jones points out in his study of Freud, the Latin *Id*, the impersonal pronoun, is meant to designate the 'non-personal part of the mind, distinct from the ego or self'. Freud, he says, thought of the id as the 'primordial reservoir of energy . . . derived from the two primary instincts'. 'It has all the negative features which Freud had previously described as characteristic of what he called the Primary System' (Jones, 1957, p. 303). Freud says that 'the pleasure-principle reigns supreme in the id'. What this comes to, he points out, is that while the individual is guided by perception and reason in those actions and responses in which the ego has a hand, those that emanate from the id are impulsive and instinctive: 'The ego represents what we call reason and sanity, in contrast to the id which contains the passions' (1949b, p. 30).

What does this amount to? First, there is the claim that 'the ego is that part of the id which has been modified by the direct influence of the external world' (1949b, p. 39). I take it that 'the influence of the external world' is meant to comprise the young child's contact and interaction with his parents and later other people in contexts provided by the culture of the society in which he grows up. It is through such contact and interaction that he acquires speech, thought, the capacity for intentional action, self-consciousness, self-control, and everything else that goes to make him an individual person. This, in Freudian terminology, is the formation of the ego. Admittedly this is a gradual process and one of the interacting parties is the ego in formation. But what does it start as? What does it bring to the interaction at the start? What does the ego develop out of?

Freud certainly considers such questions to be intelligible and his answer, in my words, is that at the beginning the young infant has neither self-consciousness nor self-control. He can neither direct his responses nor restrain them. He is not capable of thought nor, therefore, of making sense of its surroundings in terms of our adult categories of reason. Nevertheless his environment is not devoid of significance for him. What significance it has on specific occasions finds expression in his affective responses; we can see what they mean to him in these responses. Freud characterizes these responses as instinctive and they exhibit for him certain broad tendencies which he attributes to certain instincts.

It is these instincts which, in Freud's view, constitute the *content* of the id. The mode of the infant's reaction, the significance which he sees in things in his immediate environment as these affect him, the kind of primitive thought which his responses exhibit, add up to a mentality which character- izes the *form* of the id's responses. Thus on the one hand we have the instincts which Freud regards as constituting the nature common to all men, a nature which is not often observed in the raw since it is clothed, so to speak, by every- thing that man acquires in the process of civilization. On the other hand, we have a mode of thinking, assessment, and reaction which constitute a mentality in sharp conflict with the adult person's ways of deliberating and acting, one that is alien to the way he sees and thinks of himself.

Freud's view is that the instinctive impulses that belong to the id seek expression through the medium of the ego, they use it as a vehicle for their expression. The ego does not own them. Thus the fulfilment which a woman finds in mother- hood as a woman insofar as this can be distinguished from

her individual relation with her child and the personal attributes with which she enters into that relation. The claim is
that there is an impersonal aspect to what she gives of herself
and the fulfilment she finds in that giving. In this respect her
behaviour is reminiscent of that of animals — for instance,
birds raising a family and being used in the process. Under
this aspect if one describes the woman as fulfilling a purpose,
then this is her purpose not as an individual but as a woman.
Whether she flourishes or loses her youth and even perhaps
her health in the process, what she submits to is indifferent to
her welfare.

What belongs to the id is thus something to which a person
submits, it is not subject to his will. Dreams, for instance,
according to Freud come from the id, and insofar as they
express aspirations and anxieties that belong to the ego, these
are 'secondary elaborations', themselves in the service of the
wish which belongs to the id. It is this which the dream is
supposed to represent as fulfilled.

Freud, we saw, regards the id as a source of energy which
gives life to the individual, liveliness, contact with what is
alive, but which can also turn him against life, in himself as
well as in others. Putting aside the speculative aspects of his
conception of the life and death instincts, his view I think is
that a person's capacity for love and hate comes from a part
of his soul which is deeper than the part to which his reason
belongs. If he tries to cultivate his reason at its expense, if he
loses touch with it, he will dry up. He will lose his capacity
to find joy in life, to give joy to others. He will even lose his
capacity to make any sort of impression on others; they will
not notice him. Freud believes that the ego has to use this
energy, for good or ill, in acting, that it has no energy of its
own. Nothing vital or creative comes from the purely personal
level of the soul.

This is a thumb nail sketch of the salient points in Freud's
conception of the id as I see it. In it I believe, Freud focuses on
something important; but at the same time it is a conception
which raises several serious difficulties. First, the notion of a
primitive mentality that is prior to logic and civilization raises
questions which I have discussed earlier in my consideration
of the prominence given to unconscious phantasy in the

psycho-analytic conception of human life (see chapter 3 above).

Next there are difficulties in the way Freud was inclined to think of a nature common to all men irrespective of the society to which they belong and the culture in which they develop into individual human beings. Freud is right in his view that it would be wrong to think that there is nothing to man other than what in him is the product of his culture. But he is wrong in what he makes of the relation between what comes from his culture and changes a man into a 'civilized' human being, and the instinctive raw material that is thus 'transformed'. The way he thinks of the relation between the two is highly problematic and is reflected in Freud's conceptions of the id and the super-ego.

Freud's official doctrine, as expounded in *Civilization and its Discontents*, is that all men are pleasure-loving and aggressive underneath, and incapable of tolerating much frustration. Civilization in general and morality in particular are imposed on men from above and never truly become theirs. They remain a source of frustration in respect of their instinctive desires which, however plastic, are never truly transformed. On the side of the instincts men learn to act in accordance with 'the reality-principle' instead of 'the pleasure-principle', and on the side of civilization they 'internalize' the demands of morality, thus acquiring a super-ego. But the reality-principle is adopted with the aim of pursuing pleasure and instinctive gratification more successfully (see Freud, 1949d). As Freud puts it in his paper, 'Formulations Regarding the two Principles of Mental Functioning': 'The substitution of the reality-principle for the pleasure-principle denotes no dethronement of the pleasure principle, but only a safeguarding of it. A momentary pleasure, uncertain in its results, is given up, but only in order to gain in a new way an assured pleasure coming later' (1950, vol. iv, p. 18). The super-ego, on the other hand, however internal, continues to remain external to the ego and to obstruct it in its quest for the fulfilment of the id. There is a tacit assumption that it is the id which represents man's true nature and what each individual is really like underneath, behind the veneer of civilization.

I have criticized this official doctrine of Freud in *Freud and Human Nature* (chapter 6, 'Human Nature and Culture'). But I have argued that there is more to Freud's views on these matters than what is expressed in the official doctrine. Even if the id represents man's instinctive nature, his life has many dimensions not conceivable in an animal, no less real or fundamental, no less a part of him. These are not, as it were, grafted onto him, from which his instinctive nature remains separate. His instinctive reactions are extended through the new dimensions his life acquires in what he learns. They are transformed as they are taken up into actions which would not be conceivable apart from the activities in which what he learns enables him to take part, as they are directed to objects which have a significance they could never have had in earlier periods of his life.

It is true that the learning through which he grows and changes involves discipline, self-restraint and some curbing of impulses. But it doesn't follow that what is curbed is all there was to him at the start (Melanie Klein), nor that what he acquires is not as much part of him (Anderson). The change and transformation which men undergo as a result of all they learn from infancy onward is what Malinowski in *Sex and Repression in Savage Society* has described as 'the transition from nature to culture', 'from instinct to sentiment' (1955, part IV). Thus think of the way lust may be transformed into the sexual passion of love. This is a change in the person and involves the integration of what comes from the id into the ego. In the process what has its source in the id is accepted by the ego and transformed, and the ego itself is enriched. This kind of transformation takes place in the formation of moral sentiments as well.

Still Freud's view is that certain propensities remain in men, untouched by the learning which contributes to such transformation, discernable in their lives, however indirect their expression may be, directly related to their early instinctive endowment. These are what Freud tried to capture in his concept of the id. What it is meant to cover thus coincides in part with what some moral philosophers have tried to draw attention to by such notions as 'the body' or 'the flesh' − for instance, Plato in the *Phaedo*. In the *Phaedrus* he too divides the soul into three elements, and one of these, represented by a wanton black horse, is the carnal part of the soul. This, in conception, is reminiscent of Freud's id, although there are significant differences between the other two parts and the Freudian ego and super-ego.

Further questions remain. Insofar as expressions of the id form a domain in human life ruled by the kind of primitive mentality we have considered earlier, can we deny that the super-ego too partakes of this mentality? Besides, if the concept of the id is meant to bring into focus what lies beyond the conscious will of the individual, would it not also encompass the unconscious ego or, at least, some aspects of it? Freud did distinguish between these as Groddeck, from whom he borrowed the term, never does. Thus Groddeck's description of a man's choice of his profession in the first letter of *The Book of the It*. But even then, is there not at least equal justification for taking a line opposite to the one Freud took and regarding the id as an extension of the ego, as part of the self which has remained wedded to its earliest mentality? On such a view the id would become the unconscious primitive ego, a self which lacks cohesion, or one whose cohesion does not be beyond the kind captured by Professor Taylor in his concept of 'the simple weigher' discussed in the following section (see pp. 111—12).

3   The Ego and its Autonomy in Inner Conflict

If I were pressed to say what the ego is, as Freud understood it, I would say that it is the subject of intentional actions and decisions, as well as of perceptions and knowledge, the object of shame and guilt, the recipient of impulses, urges and dreams, and the sufferer of fear and anxiety. It is also involved, in logically more complex ways, in those cases where we speak of self-regard, pride, self-love and self-pity, and also self-deception, as well as of self-restraint and self-control. The concept in question is intimately connected with our use of the first person pronoun 'I' in a wide range of cases. It is in fact more or less equivalent to what we mean by 'the self' or 'selfhood'. All this is linked to what Freud says, though what he says contains various confusions:

(1) The ego as subject of intentional actions and decisions, of perceptions and knowledge. Freud spoke here of the 'functions' of the ego, much as one might speak of the functions of an organ, and listed 'perception' and 'motility' as two of these – two out of the three he usually mentions. Note the notion of 'motility' or the initiation of movements in place of 'intentional action'. But insofar as the notions of the ego or self and of human agency are interlinked, an understanding of these notions presupposes an understanding of intentional action and voluntary movement.

(2) The ego as the object of shame and guilt. Here Freud speaks of the ego being acted on by the super-ego. But this hardly advances our understanding of the responsibility which a person feels for having done something which he regards as bad or shameful, and the way his standards and values enter into the way he sees his actions and feels about what he has done. Freud speaks here of the 'functions' of the super-ego, 'self-observation' and 'criticism', meaning, presumably, reflecting on the moral character of one's actions and passing unfavourable judgments on them. He thinks of the super-ego as 'unfriendly' for its criticisms of the ego.

(3) The ego as the recipient of impulses, urges and dreams. Freud speaks of this as an aspect of the ego's relation to the id. He thinks that what is 'in the id' can find expression in consciousness only through the ego. It can find expression in action either by the consent of the ego or by the ego falling a prey to its manipulation. What we have here is the whole field of variously attenuated actions – impulsive, compulsive, unintentional, accidental, inadvertent. And we can only understand their logic by comparing them with fully intentional actions.

(4) The ego as the victim of fear and anxiety. Here Freud came to speak of anxiety as a signal of danger and he meant, I think, that anxiety is a form of apprehension; it is the anticipation of something apprehended as dangerous.

(5) In the case of self-love Freud speaks of 'narcissism'. He thinks of it as a relation of the ego with itself. He speaks of it as entailing the withdrawal of love ('libido') from other people to bestow it on oneself (1950, vol. iv, p. 33). He has interesting psychological observations to make here. But what I should like to note is that in narcissism we have one of the

few 'reflexive' phenomena Freud admits into his logical scheme. In self-hatred and self-depreciation, or masochism, for instance, we have, according to Freud, the hatred or depreciation of the ego by the super-ego. As for what Freud calls 'self-observation', we have seen that he regards the super-ego as its subject. Note that on Freud's view the ego has the 'function' of perception, while it is the super-ego which has the function of 'self-observation'. But what does Freud mean by 'self-observation': knowing what one is up to, what one has done and what one will do next, self-awareness and self-knowledge?

(6) When considering 'repression' we have seen that Freud thinks of it as something which the ego does. It does so 'in the service and at the behest of its super-ego' (1949b, p. 75). Here, on Freud's view, the ego restrains the id, refuses to give it expression in consciousness and action, in compliance with the super-ego. In ordinary self-restraint and self-control, on the other hand, it does not act in subservience to the super-ego, nor does it comply with the id. It acts on its own behalf, knowing what it is doing. Freud considers this preferable to repression: 'Where id was, there shall ego be' (1933, p. 112).

Given his way of thinking, however, this presents Freud with a difficulty. For it seems to him that it is either the id or the super-ego that can provide the ego with a motive for any action: 'The poor ego has to serve three harsh masters: the external world, the super-ego and the id' (1933, p. 108). 'In popular language', he says, 'we may say that the ego stands for reason and circumspection' (p. 107). One may compare and contrast Freud's view here with Hume's view that reason can never provide a motive for any action and must serve and obey the passions. These passions, for Freud, divide between the id and the super-ego — 'sexuality' and 'aggression'. One draws and the other pushes the ego into action. The idea of ego-instincts belong to an earlier phase of Freud's thinking. By the time he was thinking of the relations of the ego to its 'three masters' the ego-instincts were absorbed into the 'libido' which Freud thought of as 'the energy of the id'. Consequently he pictured the relation of the ego to the id as that between a rider and its horse: 'The horse provides the locomotive energy, and the rider has the prerogative of determining the goal and of guiding the movements of his powerful mount towards it' (p. 108). This is different from Hume. For in Hume the passions determine the goal or end, and reason only chooses the way or means to it.

There is still a problem for Freud here: how does the ego mediate between the incompatible demands made on it by its 'three harsh masters'? Is it merely a servant, the role of reason being confined to the keeping of peace and working out of compromises, or does it have a will of its own?

There is much in Freud that pulls him in the direction of thinking of the ego as 'a mere servant'. But, as with his 'determinism', I believe that when Freud said that 'the ego is not master in its own house' (1950, vol. iv, p. 355) he was attacking a popular naivety, not challenging 'a metaphysical assumption'. Thus we can compare the idea he was attacking with the naive view people may have, as seen in their expectations and disappointments, about people in high places who wield power and influence. One could say to them: 'Do not think that the President of the United States can get anything done he wants done or sees fit. He has to convince the men around him, persuade the Senate, get the backing of the Congress, etc. He has to do a great deal of wheeling and dealing, give concessions, plead, present his proposals in a form that will be found acceptable. Unless a lot of people are agreeable, he is thoroughly impotent.' But, of course, within this framework, he can be a weak president, placatory, doing what others tell him. He may be able to do little more than with great dexterity balance the conflicting claims and interests of the groups on whose support he depends. Or he may be a strong president, with a mind of his own, the courage of his convictions, the ability to win the agreement and enlist the support of the people he governs. Thus to say that the president 'cannot do anything he wants', 'cannot do anything on his own and without the co-operation of the Senate and the Congress' is not to deny his autonomy; it is to characterize it as a 'relative autonomy'. It is not to deny that he can act with vision and independence, that he can lead those from whom he derives his power rather than be led by them. It was the same with Freud's remark about the ego not being 'master in its own house'. It too can lead or be led by the horse it rides; but when it leads it still depends on the horse's 'loco-motive energy' as the autonomous president depends on his 'power base'.

How can the ego lead, though, without siding with one of the parties to the dispute? What does it mean for it to 'arbi-trate' in an inner conflict? Is there an independent source to its motivation? If one thinks of what is in question in everyday non-Freudian terms there are still difficulties in understanding the role of a person in the resolution of such a conflict. He may want to refrain from giving in to a desire, to control an inclination, to give up wanting what he wants. Freud repre-sents the person (ego) as helpless because he does not recog-nize the unconscious aspect of his commitments. But even if we were to imagine away this aspect of the matter, grant the person full consciousness, there is still a problem. For he is pulled in two different directions. If the balance between the conflicting pulls is stacked a certain way, how could he reverse this so that he can go one way rather than the other?

He may, for instance, be tempted by a quick and easy but dishonest way of making a large sum of money. The tempta-tion may be strong, yet he may succeed in resisting it. He may do so by turning his thoughts in a direction from which the dazzle of the money he has been offered keeps him from looking. If he can persevere, he will see the object that attracts him under a less attractive aspect. If reflection can stabilize this aspect, the attraction will decrease and he will be on the way to winning the struggle. What makes this aspect possible are his moral beliefs and the terms that belong with these. The place which these beliefs have in his life accounts for the unattractive aspect under which he can thus bring himself to see what previously attracted him. But the question is: How can he turn his thoughts in such a direction when doing so is excluded by what he wants at the time? This question, which Professor Alston raises in a paper entitled 'Self-intervention and the Structure of Motivation' (1977) is directly related to the autonomy of the Freudian ego.

Alston's solution is to distinguish between the moment of choice or commitment and the period leading up to it. At the moment of choice the disinclination to take the opportunity that tempts him must be greater if the man in our example is to resist the temptation. Yet previous to it he believes or fears that it will be otherwise. Believing this and having the moral motive, he does something to reverse what he anticipates and thus to avert the danger. Admittedly, he can only do so at a time when his sense of the danger is great and the temptation is weak; that is before the temptation invades his consciousness, displacing much else that forms part of it, i.e. his sense of the evil involved in what he is tempted to undertake. As Alston points out, while a person is in a state of conflict he is usually pulled first one way and then another; the conflicting alternatives oscillate in their appeal to him. It is this, together with his belief about the outcome of the situation if he does nothing to alter it, that make it possible for him to do something to reverse it before he is overcome.

Alston argues that two different 'motivational systems' are involved here and that there are important logical differences in the character of the desires that enter the two systems. Without going into the details of Alston's discussion, about which I have some reservations, what is important is that the desires that enter into the motivational system which Alston characterizes as 'higher' are thought-dependent. And thought is, of course, the prerogative of Freud's ego.

In another paper in the same volume, entitled 'What is Human Agency?', Professor Taylor (1977) points out that what issues confront a person depends on the way in which he can and does characterize things, think and speak about them, and that this in turn is determined in part by his values. He describes as a 'simple weigher' a man who has little regard for moral values, so that moral considerations, of one kind or another, hardly play a role in his thinking. Such a man does make choices, but he is reflective only in a minimal sense. He does weigh things before acting; he does not simply act on impulse. But the role of reflection in his life is confined to something like the following: to step back from the immediate situation, to calculate consequences, to compensate for the immediate force of one desire judged as disadvantageous to pursue, to get over hesitation by concentrating on the inarticulate 'feel' of alternatives (p. 113). Ultimately he cannot go beyond the judgment, 'This is what I like, or what I prefer to do.' It is a defect in Freud that the kind of deliberation which he attributed to the ego under the title of 'reality-testing' hardly goes beyond this minimal kind of reflection of the 'simple weigher' described by Taylor. Part of the reason for this is Freud's philosophical inability to take moral thinking seriously.

In contrast, Taylor argues, the 'strong evaluator' uses a language which enters into and makes a difference to the way he sees and experiences things and so to the world in which he lives, acts and makes decisions. He chooses a particular alternative not, as in the case of the simple weigher, because it is what *he* happens to like or want, but because of what *it* is like, characterized in terms that belong to his moral vocabulary. Therefore when he is attracted by a course of action that seems open to him, what attracts him is susceptible to reflection, and the conclusion he arrives at may make a difference to the aspect under which what is in question attracts him.

Taylor argues, further, that the norms to which the aspects under which he chooses things are responsible are themselves open to scrutiny and reflection. That is, a man may have to choose between different ways of looking at and seeing the situations that face him — ways which may be incommensurable with each other. Deliberation before acting may be 'carried on in a struggle of self-interpretations' (p. 117) — 'self-interpretations' because coming to a new perspective would be a change in the agent, an 'alteration in the ego'. Such a change would necessarily involve a change both in the direction in which a person would resolve his conflicts and also a change in the conflicts he would have to resolve. What is in question could be described as a revaluation by the individual of his values.

We see that although a person can be overcome by a desire, which at an earlier time he saw as a temptation to be resisted, and which he later comes to regret, this does not mean that such a desire cannot be resisted. Alston and Taylor explain how it can be resisted. This is not a matter of the outcome being determined by the balance of the conflicting desires, as in a dynamic system. Nor is it a matter of some 'act of will', not subject to the ordinary motives of the person, resolving the conflict. On the former view the ego would be merely a passive recipient of the conflict, with no say of its own, and so inescapably impotent. On the latter view it is above the conflict, invested with a power to resolve such conflicts that remains unintelligible because it is not related to the beliefs and desires that have become polarized in the conflict. Therefore both views are unacceptable. However they do not exhaust the field, and the possibility of self-mastery rests on the possibility of reflection *before* the person is overcome. For such reflection is responsible to the stable sentiments and deep convictions of the person, and it has the power of altering the aspect under which the alternative that tempts him appears to him. As this aspect changes so does the attraction it exercises on the person.

This is the gist of the *philosophical* resolution offered regarding the ego's autonomy in inner conflict. But whether or not the ego can actually play an effective role in any given case would depend on its strength — with all that this involves in developmental terms.[1] Here Freud had a distinctive contribution to make — one that was to be further developed by later psycho-analysts.

4   The Ego in its Relations with the Id and the Super-ego

The ego, then, has the capacity to reflect on, evaluate and revaluate, the demands that are made on it by the id, the super-ego, and the environment — circumstances, social conventions, other people. It can face these demands from a position of strength or from a position of weakness. In each case there are two alternatives open to it. From a position of strength it can endorse or repudiate such a demand. When it endorses it, it acts on its own behalf. When it repudiates it, it does so on the basis of values or long-term goals which it has made its own. From a position of weakness it complies with such a demand in a placatory way or hides from it — by resorting to repression or reaction-formation. Here it does

---

[1] One kind of weakness of the ego relevant to our present discussions is the one we refer to as 'weakness of the will'. See chapter 10, section 5 below.

not act on its own behalf, whether the line it takes is repressive or submissive. Whichever way the ego faces the 'inner' demands made upon it, it will duplicate this in its relations with the outside world.

Repression and other forms of control and defence are thus expressions of weakness of the ego. Freud speaks of repression as something which the ego does 'in the service and at the behest of its super-ego'. In other words, here the ego restrains the id in compliance with the super-ego, whereas in ordinary self-restraint it acts on its own behalf, knowing what it is doing (see Freud, 1949a, p. 248). Here there is no division of will. Thus where a person forgoes doing something that attracts him for the sake of someone he loves, for instance, he does not do so under threat, or because he is afraid to incur anyone's displeasure or disapproval. Giving up what attracts him is what *he* wants to do. Under its new aspect what attracted him loses its attraction. And even where something of the original attraction remains, the light in which it appears gives him sufficient reason for him to want to give it up, given the things he cares for, so that he is still fully behind his choice not to go after it. What unifies his will, or keeps it one, is his love and deep regard for the person for whose sake he gives it up. Or it may be his genuine belief in the values which cast an unfavourable light upon the object that attracted him.

Thus when the ego repudiates a demand made by the id, it derives its strength and sustenance from certain feelings and sentiments. These, in the above example, are the person's love for someone he cares for, or his regard for values in which he believes. In other words, if we identify the ego here with reason, we could say that it does not rule at the expense of the passions, but with their consent and, indeed, with their support.

Earlier I said that when Freud says that 'the ego is not master in its own house' he is thinking of its subservience to its 'three harsh masters', but that he would have said that even when not subservient the ego's autonomy is a relative autonomy. When it leads it still depends on the 'locomotive energy' of its mount in the way that the autonomous president depends on his 'power base'. The president, if he is to lead, has to be in touch with, understand and respect the different shades of opinion that give him the basis of his power. Similarly, the ego cannot act without regard to its moral beliefs and its emotions without alienating them. When Freud says that the ego is not 'master' he means that it is not an absolute monarch. He is opposing an omnipotent conception of reason — such as, for instance, we find in Kant.

There is a difference between the ego acting in subservience to its super-ego and a person obeying the voice of his conscience in particular circumstances. In the former case the person may be acting out of a fear of punishment, his main concern being to placate an over-strict conscience. In the latter case his conscience reminds him of what he himself believes, so that in heeding it he acts out of genuine conviction and so is fully behind what he does. There is a similar difference between the ego acting in subservience to its id, giving way to impulses of lust, for instance, and its endorsing some powerful emotion. Only in the latter case will the emotion be consolidated into a genuine affective relationship in the context of which the ego is fully behind the actions it undertakes. That is when the ego is not subservient, it is not the case that it dictates. Rather it carries along with it aspects of the personality which are themselves transformed in this new relationship with the ego.

In fact, domination and subservience constitute a dichotomy only from a common basis of weakness, where domination is a 'reaction-formation'. Thus Freud suggests that, broadly speaking, there are three possible relations in which the ego or reason can stand to the id or the passions. (a) It can try to make itself independent of the emotions, reject their contribution as dangerous and corrupting, and see its role as being to tame and subdue them. The conception of reason which such a relation is likely to nurture is reminiscent of the rationalistic conception of reason. I say 'reminiscent', and not identical, because I take the kind of conception at the core of rationalism to have a life in a movement of thought capable of standing on its own feet. Whereas here it is the 'rationalization' of an ego that is the plaything of passions that belong to the super-ego. What rules here is not reason but a semblance of it. (b) The ego or reason can enter into the service of the passions. The conception of reason here is reminiscent of romanticism, which views reason as the enemy of life and believes that a full life can only be found in submitting to the passions. These two conceptions of reason, the omnipotent and the negativistic conceptions, are two views of the same thing seen from opposite ends — the same thing being a reason that has come to be dissociated from the emotions. (c) The ego or reason can enlist the support of the emotions, derive sustenance and vitality from them, or as Freud puts it 'borrow' their energy. This calls for their 'integration' rather than their 'repression', and this involves the transformation in certain respects of both reason and the emotions in the direction of an increase in the person's autonomy. Freud sums it up in his formula: 'Where id was, there ego shall be.'

There is a counterpart to each of these three relations in the case of the super-ego. (a) The ego or reason can try to make itself independent of the super-ego, thinking of morality on the model of *its* (the super-ego's) demands, rejecting it as arbitrary conventions that can have no basis in reason, except a purely prudential one. This is reminiscent of a form of rationalism which regards morality as a kind of superstition. Freud's own thinking was in fact influenced by such a conception (see Dilman, 1983, chapter 4). (b) It can enter into the service of the super-ego, making its every word his command. Here we have the seeds of a form of moralism which is antithetical to a genuine moral attitude (see the example discussed in chapter 11 below). (c) The third alternative is one on which Melanie Klein and her followers have focused attention and illuminated. On their view the super-ego has a positive aspect in addition to the negative one emphasized by Freud. It contains love as well as inverted aggression and is thus capable of entering into a co-operative relationship with the ego. To enlist the support of this aspect of the super-ego involves the ego in tolerating guilt and depression. If it can do so, not only will the original demands of the super-ego be transformed, so that the person finds a new relationship with an outside morality,[2] but he will also find a

---

[2] By an 'outside' morality I mean one that exists independently of him, one which he may come to accept and make his own.

greater concern for other people and a richer relationship with them. This is what Winch hints at (1968, p. 12) when he says of Ibsen's character Mrs Solness that 'if she had occasionally forgotten her "duty" and let herself go, this might have cleared the air and opened the way for some genuine human relationships'.[3]

5   Freud and Melanie Klein on the Super-ego

Freud makes a close connection between the super-ego and conscience. But I would say that the super-ego is to conscience what the kind of mentality which characterizes the id is to adult reason and common sense. The super-ego is the father's voice, or anyone else's who stood to the young child in the role of the disciplinarian, assimilated by the child. It is, however, not the father's voice as he spoke in reality, but as the child heard it at the time and still hears it as an adult. It has a character which comes largely from the child's anger towards and fear of his father. It is a voice harsh with the anger it mirrors and, therefore, one to be feared. What is at the centre of Freud's doctrine here is the way we retain figures from the past, coloured and distorted by our emotions, so that while they become part of ourselves they nevertheless keep a certain independence, guiding and bullying us. We cannot ignore their demands, yet in heeding them we are not entirely ourselves and do not act fully on our own behalf.

Melanie Klein held that the super-ego is formed much earlier than Freud claimed. The further back we go in its history the less does it resemble anything that we call conscience. It was the way the super-ego can provide the ego with an ideal to emulate which gave Freud the idea of a link between it and conscience. To what extent what it provides is an 'ideal' in the moral sense is questionable. But, in any case, this aspect is almost completely absent in the earlier stages of its development. There what is most prominent are persecution and reciprocal fear.

---

[3] I shall say more about the kind of transformation anticipated in Winch's words in chapter 11 below.

The super-ego, then, is a primitive or archaic part of our mind which survives in the unconscious. Freud thought it worthwhile to single it out for study and to mark it with a name because of the prominent part it plays in such pathological conditions as paranoia and melancholia, as well as in more normal behaviour in which cruelty, self-abasement and obsessive scrupulosity pass for moral behaviour. Many psychoanalysts have distinguished it from conscience. Erich Fromm, for instance, in *Man for Himself* represents the distinction as one between two forms of conscience — 'authoritarian' and 'humanistic conscience'. There is much in what he says that I would criticize; but the main point of interest for us now is his observation that what he calls 'authoritarian conscience' is the 'conscience' of a man who (as I would put it) is only *externally* related to the values which enter his judgments and actions: 'The prescriptions of authoritarian conscience are not determined by one's own value judgments but exclusively by the fact that its commands and taboos are pronounced by authorities' (1950, pp. 144—5). Fromm describes 'humanistic conscience' as a person's 'own voice' as opposed to 'the internalized voice of an authority' (p. 158).

In 'Psycho-analysis and Ethics' Money-Kyrle uses the same words, 'authoritarian' and 'humanistic conscience', but the distinction he makes derives from Melanie Klein's work. Again, I would not go along with everything he says here. However I should like to single out his distinction between 'persecutory' and 'depressive' guilt — a guilt based on fear and one based on love. The former is the prerogative of an 'authoritarian' conscience. In the earliest stages of infancy the expectation of harsh treatment is the expectation of retaliation for the bad feelings and savage phantasies provoked in the child by frustration, hunger and discomfort. This fear of retaliation is the earliest prototype of guilt and is the precursor of the super-ego which Freud describes as 'the heir of the Oedipus complex'.

In Melanie Klein's view 'the super-ego does not begin about the age of five, but is already at that age approaching its final form after five years of previous development' (Money—Kyrle, 1955, p. 431). But it is not this that is really new in Melanie Klein's contribution. What is new is her introduction of a different form of guilt into the child's early affective life and relationships, one neglected by Freud, namely depressive guilt, and restitutive and reparative responses. Depressive guilt is the child's reaction of dismay at realizing that the mother with whom he has been enraged and whom he has destroyed in his phantasies is the very same person whom he loves dearly. This realization evokes in the child feelings of a depressive character, guilt and dismay, of which being sorry is a later and more sophisticated variety. Melanie Klein would say that being sorry is not something that the child is taught, though saying 'I am sorry' is. It is a primitive reaction at having spoilt, hurt or done harm to something or someone that is dear to him. She would say that the mother's role as 'educator' is not to teach it but to create conditions favourable to its development.

Experiences that undermine the child's confidence in himself and trust in others, those that promote fear and anxiety in him, those that provoke rage and anger, will diminish his capacity to feel depressive guilt. The ground will thus be laid for the consolidation of the kind of 'conscience' or quasi-moral mentality Freud calls the super-ego. Melanie Klein points out that the aggressive and destructive tendencies which go into the building up of the super-ego are actually reduced by experiences which promote love and trust. For seeing the reflection of friendly qualities in other people 'reduces persecutory anxiety' (Klein, 1952, p. 208). The ability to make reparation decreases depression. Thus she speaks of the 'progressive assimilation of the super-ego by the ego' (p. 214).

Such 'assimilation', whether it takes place in the course of a person's development or is helped along by analysis, involves the reduction of what may be called 'secondary' fear and anger, and the 'working through' of guilt and depression, as the person is able to make up for the hurtful tendencies that emanate from him. For instance, he may come to be able to say 'I am sorry' and 'Thank you' with greater readiness, and not in a placatory way, to say these things and mean them. When these words come from fear or anxiety they are the expression of defensive postures. But the love or concern from which they may also come is antithetical to self-defence.

It is central to both Freud's and Melanie Klein's thought that resorting to defensive measures locks an individual's emotional development in a vicious circle.

Once, however, the hold of this circle has been weakened, the rest can come from the individual. This involves waiting and not running away, enduring anxiety, grief, guilt and depression. But this is very different from wallowing in misery, trying to make capital of it. For that too is an evasion, an attempt to reduce the pain by turning it into an advantage. This process of 'working through' is what I am inclined to describe as the integration of the love which the person has into the will. Freud spoke of this as the replacement of repression with self-mastery. As Melanie Klein puts it: 'This new capacity to feel concern for his objects helps him (the infant) to learn gradually to control his impulses' (Segal, 1964, p. 61). It is interesting that Winnicott calls Melanie Klein's 'depressive position' 'the stage of concern'.

In his book *The Survival of English* Ian Robinson comments on the trivialization of sex characteristic of our times and criticizes a 'modern' attitude towards guilt: 'The removal of the possibility of guilt is the removal of the possibility of significance' (1975, p. 189). This possibility of significance is bound up with the possibility of concern. The values which provide the framework within which this concern develops come to the individual from outside, from the life of the society to which they belong. They have the power to beget new responses and sentiments in the individual. Nevertheless, it is equally true, as Melanie Klein and others have stressed, that the root of this concern or love lies within the individual and manifests itself in early reactions to other people, notably the mother, which do not have to be taught.

What the 'modern' attitude confuses in its opposition to guilt is 'persecutory' and 'depressive' guilt; and the reduction of the former would neither constitute the removal of 'the possibility of significance', nor would it promote 'licence'. As Melanie Klein puts it: 'In mitigating the severity of the super-ego by lessening the operation of its sadistic constituents . . . analysis prepared the way not only for the achievement of social adaptability in the child, but for the development of moral and ethical standards in the adult' (1948, p. 73). In this way the super-ego 'gradually becomes transformed into conscience in the true sense of the word' (p. 68).

This is the other aspect of the enlargement of the self which Freud indicated by the formula: 'Where id was, there ego shall be.' Here he could have said: 'Where super-ego was, there ego shall be.' What is in question involves the will. Passions and desires that are external to the will are transformed into stable sentiments and integrated into new dispositions of the will.

6   Integration of the Self

When Freud theorized about the divisions of the personality he was not speaking about something that is immutable. He was attempting to express certain 'dissociations' within the personality which are significant from the standpoint of his therapeutic work. They can be healed, but not completely irradicated.

What is in question are at once real dissociations in the personality and also polarities of the mind, co-ordinates for plotting men's inner conflicts in a way which makes easy comparisons possible. The dissociations are, of course, subject to change, while the polarities are immutable insofar as they are aspects of a mode of representation. In this latter respect we can compare Freud's model for 'the structure of the personality' with Plato's picture of the divisions of the soul in the *Phaedrus* already mentioned.

Plato was primarily concerned with the conflict between good and evil within the soul and the varying degrees of autonomy men are capable of attaining in their struggle to come to terms with such a conflict. Freud too, we have seen, is interested in the question of man's autonomy and the conditions that are favourable to its development, although his interest does not have the spiritual orientation which characterizes Plato's philosophy. Plato, like Freud, divides the soul into three elements and uses the analogy of the rider and his horse. In fact, he compares the relation between the three elements to a charioteer and his two horses. In this analogy the emotions and desires are divided between the two horses which represent the carnal and the spiritual aspects of the soul. That is, while Plato holds that reason can enable us to control certain of our passions, and must do so, there is no question of its ruling the soul, as in Kant, at the expense of the passions in general. Where reason is dissociated from the passions it cannot rule the soul, for it is the horses which propel the chariot. What rules the soul in such a case is only the semblance of reason — and if Plato had our modern term he would have spoken here of 'rationalization'.

Freud would have agreed. He would have said that here reason has become a slave of certain passions. However, although Freud too divides the soul, or the mind as he prefers to call it, into three elements, he is unable to represent what is higher there. For he identifies it with the super-ego which is largely an embodiment of restrictions, reaction-formations, compensations and, at best, idealizations (1933, pp. 82, 95). There is, then, little correspondence, at first sight, between Freud's super-ego, with aggression as its energy, and Plato's white horse whose 'thirst for honour is tempered by restraint and modesty' (1973b, p. 62). We have seen how Melanie Klein was able to remedy this defect.[4]

There seems to be equally little correspondence, at first sight, between Freud's ego, represented as harassed from all sides and the servant of three harsh masters, and Plato's charioteer who, while at the mercy of a wanton black horse, still has the support of a white horse who 'needs no whip, but is driven simply by the word of command' (Plato, 1973b, p. 62). Also this charioteer, who represents reason, is sustained by the vision of ideals to which, unlike Hume's reason, he is not indifferent. Their vision dazzles his eyes. We have seen, however, that when Freud speaks of the ego as a servant, it is the possibility of its absolute autonomy that he wishes to deny.

Freud holds, I argued, that the ego can achieve relative autonomy if it is prepared to give the demands of the id and the super-ego due consideration. Otherwise it would alienate itself from the sources of life to be found in these two direc-

---

[4] For a fuller treatment of this question see Dilman, 1983, chapter 5, 'Love and Morality'.

tions. His view is that it is what the ego has retained of its early good relationships that sustains it in its transactions with the id and the super-ego — transactions in which what remains split from the ego in the id and super-ego are integrated with the ego and transformed in the process. Thus the formation of stable moral sentiments which make up a basis for action, the establishment of affective relationships which become a new source of life. As the domain of the ego is thus enlarged — and this means thoughtful, intentional action which makes sense to the person — the ego becomes stronger and more confident.

By 'strength of the ego' Freud did not mean the capacity to impose one's will on others. When he said 'where id was, there ego shall be', he was not thinking of the ego 'taking over the id'. He said that when a person advances in this direction 'he loses some of his ego' (Wortis, 1954, p. 80). He meant that he is freed from the need to assert himself, and he is no longer afraid to let go. He can give himself to activities that absorb his interest, lose himself in moments of joy or grief. Freud sees this capacity of the ego to abandon itself as an expression of the ego's strength and its lack of narcissism. He believed that (a) when the ego stops loving itself and turns its love and interest outwards, and (b) when it accepts the id and makes peace with the super-ego, it can make deeper contact with the outside world — with the activities going on around him, with the people engaged in them, with their concerns, and with other features of his environment.

The person whose ego is at one with these other aspects of himself, that is, the person who is at one with himself, has greater freedom to use his reason in the context of activities and relationships in which he finds interest and pleasure. Both his reason and his feelings are accessible to him, and they are accessible to him not as two separate things to be combined, as in Hume, but as one thing, as this finds expression in his responses to particular situations and questions.

Thus in Freud autonomy can be achieved neither at the expense of the passions, by repression, not at the expense of one's moral beliefs and sentiments, in licence. It calls for an integration of these to the ego, and this is an enlargement of the self. We shall see in the following chapter that it is in this enlargement that the self finds knowledge of itself, an enlargement which involves the integration of what is old and the assimilation of what is new. The former is what has remained dissociated, while the latter is what comes from outside.

8

Self-knowledge: Autonomy and Authenticity

In his *Introductory Lectures*, speaking about the 'inner change' which psycho-analytic therapy aims at, Freud says: 'A neurotic who has been cured has really become a different person, although at bottom of course he remains the same — that is, he has become his best self, what he would have been under the most favourable conditions' (1949a, pp. 363—4). He says that the analyst aims at bringing about such a change by 'making conscious the unconscious, removing repressions, filling in the gaps in memory' (p. 363).

Freud does not equate this with self-knowledge. We have seen that the becoming conscious of what is unconscious is a change in the person (see chapter 4, section 4, above). But the 'inner change' which Freud speaks of in the above passage goes beyond that. It is a change that involves the 'growth of the self'. Hence Freud's reference to 'what he (the neurotic) would have been under the most favourable conditions' — that is, conditions which would not have thwarted or arrested his development.

We often speak here of a person 'finding himself' or 'becoming himself'. Such a person should not be confused with the man who 'shows his true colour' and so may also be described as 'having become himself'. The latter may, for instance, show himself to be the cheat and the liar that he is. Here we cannot speak of either 'emotional growth' or 'authenticity', and there is no paradox in saying that to the extent to which he reveals his dishonesty he has shed some of his dishonesty. At least he no longer pretends to be a better man than he is. But this does not so far make him a better man or a more honest person.

If, however, the dishonesty in question is something about which he has deceived *himself*, then in coming to acknowledge it he becomes more honest with himself. Since he has deceived himself about it, presumably he finds the knowledge of it painful. So he will not like what he comes to see in himself. Therefore either he will in time come to stop disliking it or he will stop being dishonest — he will come to see that he cannot cheat those he cares for without hurting himself. In either case we have a change in the person, the one change being in the opposite direction from the other. The former change, insofar as it involves coming to endorse a life of dishonesty, is a change away from authenticity. However, the man who comes to acknowledge his own dishonesty will normally change in the opposite direction. For he will want to do something about it and, given a little more courage, he will try.

Freud takes this for granted in the form of therapy he has developed. Such therapy, in any case, presupposes at least a modicum of honesty in the analysand who is asked to tell the analyst what comes to his head without any reservation or distortion. It also presupposes a dissatisfaction with the way he is, a dissatisfaction which embraces the way he relates himself to other people. Freud believes that the process of facing what one finds painful in oneself, and for that reason avoided recognizing, will lead to the kind of 'inner change' which is a development of the self towards greater autonomy and authenticity.[1] This is what he understands by 'self-knowledge'.

Here the antithesis of what he and others have called 'knowledge' is not false belief, but naivity, immaturity or self-deception. Thus consider why we would not attribute self-knowledge to a child. Certainly not because of any truths about himself which he does not know, but because he is as

---

[1] It will do so, Freud believed, because there is in most people a propensity towards growth, a desire for honesty, a concern for other people, all of which Freud gathers under 'the life instinct'. He later came to question this presupposition in his paper 'Analysis Terminable and Interminable' — see 1950, vol. v.

yet far from wisdom and maturity. These are what characterize the self, the way he *is*, not the beliefs he holds about
himself.

There is not a single antithesis to self-knowledge; but one
that I mentioned is self-deception. Obviously a person who
deceives himself, to the extent to which he does so, lacks
self-knowledge. To come to self-knowledge here means for
him to stop deceiving himself. Yet it is notorious that, by and
large, philosophers have discussed this notion in terms of
belief. To be deceived (they said) is to have false beliefs.
Therefore to be self-deceived is to have a false belief about
oneself, one which hides an unwelcome truth and which one
has sought for that reason. This may well be so, but it is not
the only kind of case where we speak of self deception (see
Dilman and Phillips, 1971, chapters 3—4).

There are many cases, relevant to our present discussion,
where stopping to deceive oneself, and so coming to self-
knowledge, is not merely a change in one's beliefs about
oneself, but a change in oneself from falsity to truthfulness.
This latter is inseparable from honesty with other people, the
will and the ability to form honest relationships with them.
Thus self-knowledge, though it does require that one's beliefs
about oneself be true, also requires that they be held honestly.
This honesty characterizes the person's will — the way he
enters into the things he does and the convictions he holds
about what is important and valuable.

Thus a person whose convictions about what matters are
little more than part of his childhood cargo, or conversely,
one in whom such convictions do not draw sustenance from
something that is rooted in his past, will hardly know what to
make of what he meets in life. He will not be able to enter
fully into the things he does, the activities in which he
engages. His engagements will not be one of whole-hearted
commitment (hence Erich Fromm speaks of 'alienation' here).
The possibility of his learning and growing through these
activities will be limited. We shall not be able to say that they
receive his full support, that he gives his best to them, nor
that he finds great sustenance in them. What such a person
wants out of life will not be clear to him. Though it may
seem that he wants little or that he gets just what he wants,

this will be an illusion. There are many defences which such a person has to give up before he feels lost and in such loss grasps the opportunity to find himself and so come to self-knowledge.

This coming to know what one wants, which is at the centre of coming to know oneself, needs to be distinguished from coming to recognize one's desires and appetites. That someone has the desires which he has 'repressed' is a fact about him which awaits his discovery. If, on the other hand, we say of him that he now 'knows what he wants', or that he has 'found himself', this does not mean that there was something there waiting to be discovered. Leonardo da Vinci compared the way the painter and the sculptor work. The former, he said, works *per via di porre*, that is by applying a substance, particles of colour, on the colourless canvas, whereas the sculptor proceeds in the opposite direction and works *per via di levare*, or by removing, taking away from the rough stone all that hides the surface of the statue contained in it. Freud borrowed this analogy in contrasting psycho-analysis with suggestive therapy: 'The technique of suggestion aims in a similar way at proceeding *per via di porre*; . . . it superimposes something — a suggestion . . . Analytic therapy, on the other hand, does not seek to add or introduce anything new, but to take away something, to bring out something' (1950, vol. i, pp. 253–4). I mention this now in order to bring out the difference between becoming aware of 'repressed' desires and coming to know what one wants.

Freud was certainly concerned to promote the latter, but he did not always recognize the difference and he sometimes spoke as if all that there is to self-knowledge is the discovery of 'the contents of one's unconscious mind'. To come to such knowledge the analysand has to stop evading it. Doing so is a change in the attitudes, modes of thinking and responses which make up the face which he shows the world and with which he faces everyday life. It is a change in the way he *appears*, primarily to himself. It reveals him to himself.

The analyst, then, enables the analysand to *shed* what he clings to defensively (works *per via di levare*) so that he can himself face what he has been avoiding. It is in this way that what is unconscious becomes conscious. Not through receiving, from the analyst, true beliefs about himself. This would not amount to knowledge. Otherwise, as Freud pointed out, the analysand may just as well go to lectures or read books on psycho-analysis (1950, vol. ii, p. 302). He would then acquire something second-hand; whereas psycho-analysis aims at freeing him to make these discoveries for himself. Here there *is* something waiting to be discovered. But such discovery is not the end of the road to self-knowledge, it is the beginning. For now the analysand can look for a way in life and make something of himself in it. It is this which gives him the opportunity to 'become his best self', an opportunity which in the past he exchanged for safety and security. Facing unpalatable facts about himself, I am suggesting, enables him to find himself, because avoiding doing so keeps him from the kind of exploration and outward movement necessary to finding what he wants, what he can put his heart into. To repeat, facing these facts about himself does not constitute self-knowledge. But it brings into his relationship with himself the kind of honesty without which there can be no development towards self-knowledge.

I said that if in the end we can say of him that he now 'knows what he wants', or that he has 'found himself', this does not mean that there was something there waiting to be discovered. Neither is the sculpture 'in' the rough stone in this sense, waiting to be discovered. But this does not prevent us from speaking of a 'discovery' by the creative artist when he says, 'This is the right shape, configuration, colour or word – the one I have been looking for all along.' The discovery here belongs to the creation and is responsible to a particular tradition. Just as 'finding' what one wants is making something of oneself. Neither is something arbitrary.

Some philosophers have talked of 'decision' here. This is the kind of decision that enters one's most basic beliefs – beliefs about what is important and worthwhile. But the attitude of will at the heart of these beliefs is not something one chooses, although it is subject to reflection and revision in certain circumstances. It involves one's responsibility in that one endorses the values in question *oneself*, or one evades doing so. And until one endorses them one is not a moral agent in the full sense – which does not mean that one

is not responsible for what one does, that others are not
justified in holding one accountable. There are degrees of
evasion, of course, but one who evades making one's moral
belief's one's own is a man who has no bearings and who may
be said not to know what he wants. He plays at the things he
does, for instance, or he does them for the sake of appearances. Or he throws himself into projects to avoid facing the
void left in him by his lack of conviction. The latter is akin
to Kafka's 'complete citizen' who 'travels over the sea in a
ship with foam before him and wake behind, that is, with
much effect round about'. But, as Kafka points out, he is in
reality no different from 'the man in the waves on a few
planks of wood that even bump against and submerge each
other'. 'For he and his property are not one, but two, and
whoever destroys the connection destroys him at the same
time' (Kafka, 1948, p. 25).

It is at such extremes that the question, 'What do I want?'
shades into the question, 'Who am I?' The search to which
these questions are a prelude involves a decision — the decision
to give up something, to stop pretending, and eventually to
give oneself to certain things. We may finally be able to say
of him that he has *found* himself or that he has come to
know himself. The two expressions are equivalent. I spoke of
'decision'. What is in question is more like a turning around.
In the case of the man who plays at the things he does, or the
one who submerges himself into busy activities, this may
amount to dropping the pretence or standing still. This turning
around from movement to stillness is a resolve to do without
protection. If he can live through the anguish to which it
leaves him exposed he may come to something more genuine
in himself and find something he can make better sense of
and give himself to.

Compare with the case of a man who is caught up in a
moral dilemma, doesn't know what to do or which way to
go. What he is looking for is a resolution to his dilemma.
Surely a decision that resolves it need not be 'irresponsible'
or 'arbitrary'. It can be the right decision for him to take, or
the wrong one. But if right, it has to be *creative*: it has to
open up or lay down a path, not find one that is already
there. Still, obviously, not any path will do; it must be one he

will find acceptable, one he can follow. Others must be able to recognize that when he says he finds it acceptable he is not fooling himself. In some ways his decision is like a judge's verdict which, though informed by a consideration of past verdicts in parallel cases, nevertheless creates a precedent and innovates the law. It hits the right chord and is accepted by jurists. In the moral case what the decision innovates is the person; and it can only do so if it is right. For this it must be intelligible to those who share the agent's values, though it need not be one they would take in the agent's place. Obviously it must be accepted by the agent. This is what makes it a 'discovery'. If it is wrong, the change in the person constitutes self-deception.

So there are two different kinds of case in which a person may be said not to know what he wants — though we do not use the same expressions to talk about them. (a) 'He wants to do such-and-such, but he doesn't know *that* he wants it.' This is the kind of case where Freud talks of the unconscious and refers to repressed desires. (b) 'He doesn't know *what* he wants.' This is where coming to the knowledge in question involves what I called a turning around. Accordingly, there are two forms of self-deception which should not be confused with each other. (a) In the one case a person avoids facing or acknowledging some truth about himself which he finds unpalatable. He has, therefore, false beliefs for which he is responsible in the sense that he clings to them and is unwilling to give them up. (b) In the other case the deception consists not in the person having a false belief about himself, but in his being false. He is not deceived in his beliefs about himself, but in himself. In the former case, where a person is deceived in his beliefs, to be self-deceived he must not only be the victim of the deception, but also its agent. He must actively avoid recognizing the falsity of his beliefs, cling to them defensively. For he can suffer the deception without participating in its creation or maintenance — in which case he would be merely deceived, without being self-deceived. This is not possible where he is deceived in himself. For there the deception lies in the things for which he lives and the ends he pursues. It is in being behind these things that he is self-deceived. This is one kind of case. But it is not one where I would say,

'He doedn't know what he wants'. In the *Gorgias* Socrates
talks of such a man as 'not doing what he wills' (see Dilman,
1979, chapter 3, section 2) and one example that comes up
in discussion is the case of Archelaus.

There are two kinds of case where we may describe a man
as 'false' in himself. In one case he is false because he is not
himself, is other than he *is*; in the other case he is false because
he is other than what he *ought* to be. In the latter case we are
making a value judgment to which the man himself does not
subscribe. Thus he has himself no moral reservations about
the ends he has made his own: pleasure, power and prestige.
I said in *Sense and Delusion* that I would speak of self-deception here only if the person in question was one who rejected
all moral perspective; such a person remains 'insensible to a
whole dimension of reality' (Dilman and Phillips, 1971,
p. 90). Necessarily his personality would lack a whole dimension. For there is an internal connection between a person's
mode of affective response and the kind of self he possesses,
the kind of person he is.

In 'What is Human Agency?' Taylor discusses the sense in
which the kind of person I have just referred to has a *stunted*
self. He does not use this expression, but speaks of 'different
kinds of selves which strong and weak evaluation involves'
(1977, p. 112). He is concerned with the difference which
moral values make to human life and the individuals who live
that life. Thus a person who has no regard for any absolute
moral value lacks depth. Certain kinds of consideration do
not worry him at all. He is reflective, but only in a minimal
sense. His life largely consists of using and manipulating other
people; give-and-take is based for him on the satisfaction of
mutual interests. Obviously he does weigh things before acting
and does not simply act on impulse. But the role of reflection
in his life is confined in the way we have noted in the previous
chapter. As we have seen, ultimately he cannot go beyond
the judgment: 'This is what I like or what I prefer to do.' He
may regret what he does, but he is incapable of self-criticism
in the full sense. There is no place for remorse in his life, no
room for ideals that measure him and with which he can strive
to come to the right relation. The categories of the terrible
and the tragic do not enter into his conception of life.

In contrast Taylor's 'strong evaluator', the man who has moral beliefs, can articulate the superiority of the alternatives he chooses, for he has a language of contrastive characterization (1977, p. 113). He chooses a particular alternative not, as in the case of Taylor's 'simple weigher', because it is what *he* happens to like, want or prefer, but because of what *it* is like, characterized in terms that belong to his evaluative language. So Taylor describes him as possessing 'articulacy', 'depth' and the capacity for a 'plurality of visions'. He does not only choose between this or that, but also between alternatives that present themselves to him as 'higher' and 'lower' — that is, in terms that belong to his moral vocabulary. He may also have to choose between different ways of looking at and seeing the situation that faces him, ways that may be incommensurable with each other. Such deliberation involves a struggle between different modes of 'self-interpretation', modes of interpretation which determine the place on which the person stands as an individual and so affect his very identity: 'The notion of identity refers to certain evaluations which are essential because they are the indispensable horizon or foundation out of which we reflect and evaluate as persons' (p. 125).

What Socrates says in the *Gorgias* about the man whose life is single-mindedly devoted to the pursuit of pleasure is reminiscent of Taylor. He argues that exclusive devotion to pleasure uproots an individual from all sources of sustenance in life. It takes the place of the commitments from which a man can act and make sense of things. This is the centre that gives substance and unity to the self. Without it a man is but a shadow and the self is stamped with unreality. The reality it lacks is moral in character, but when we describe him as 'stunted' we do not speak from the point of view of any *particular* moral value. As I said, his life is closed to a whole dimension of reality and this characterizes the kind of self he possesses, the kind of person he is.

This connects with what Freud says in the passage I quoted at the beginning of this chapter. When he speaks there of a man becoming 'what he would have been under the most favourable conditions' he is referring to conditions that would have furthered his development, instead of stunting it. I am not suggesting that a person whose development has been stunted is necessarily self-deceived. He need not be; but he lacks self-knowledge. As I said earlier, self-knowledge has many antitheses: immaturity is one of them. Certainly psycho-analytic treatment does aim at uncovering and unlocking inner conflict so that the analysand can continue to develop unhindered. Such development involves the deployment of faculties which were previously in the service of one-sided goals.

I am claiming that there is an important connection between emotional and moral maturity and self-knowledge. Thus an emotionally immature person may well know or recognize his proclivities, but this does not justify us in describing him as possessing self-knowledge. I said that we would not speak of a child as having self-knowledge. For his faculty of self-criticism has not and cannot as yet have developed, and there is a whole world of experience and response that has not opened to him. By 'self-criticism' I refer to an attitude of mind which is the opposite of naive, one that is content to take things on trust and at face value. A person who is self-critical has had his eyes opened to the pitfalls and difficulties involved in being oneself in what one does and in keeping faith with what one believes in. This does not mean necessarily that he can imagine and formulate objections to taking the various alternatives that present themselves to him or articu-late their significance. There is a perfectly good sense in which he may know all this and so be wise to it — e.g. he may recog-nize what is objectionable when he meets it, may not be fooled, be able to anticipate his own objections and so avoid the snares of temptation. Yet he may not be able to represent these to himself in advance and so lack the ability to conduct criticism. In that sense he may be 'inarticulate' without lack-ing the frame of mind I described as 'self-critical'.

I mention this because there is a danger of equating self-criticism with a kind of articulacy one might expect to find in a philosopher or at least in someone intellectually educated. Taylor comes near to falling into this trap. He discusses that aspect of self-criticism he calls 'radical evaluation', that is the revaluation of one's values, in other words the very basis of one's moral judgments and decisions. He argues, rightly, not only that this is possible, but also that without such a possibility a person cannot be *at one* with the values that enter his moral judgments and decisions. And if he were not, then of course his judgments would be second-hand and he would not be acting on his own behalf. Unless this is the case, he cannot be himself and so cannot be said to have self-knowledge. In his discussion of the kind of self-criticism that changes the agent's perspective and identity, Taylor puts great stress on the way the language which the person speaks enlarges his horizons and determines what it is possible for him to see and understand and so the kind of person he is capable of being.

When Taylor speaks of the 'articulacy' of the 'strong evaluator', the moral agent, he is thinking of a capacity which is internal to his possession of the diverse categories that belong to a language such as we speak. In contrast, the 'simple weigher' lacks the language of certain distinctions, or at least it does not play a role in his life. He cannot think these distinctions or sees no point in availing himself of them, and so they do not exist for him, or at least they do not possess any reality for him — they are not part of the world in which he lives and acts. When I say that a man may be 'inarticulate' although he has emerged from naivity and a life of habit or compliance, I am not using the term 'articulate' in Taylor's sense, but in its common meaning. In that meaning a person may be 'inarticulate' just because he is unable to express himself in the language he possesses. He has the language, its life is in his veins, but he lacks command of it. Such a man, I am saying, can be thoughtful and critical in that he is not easily fooled, although he is not a thinker. His thoughtfulness, in the sense of what he heeds and is aware of, is manifest in his life and actions, in the independence of his decisions and in the way he keeps to them, although he is no good at arguing things, at setting them out in general terms. He does not carry out any 'radical evaluation', yet he may be receptive, open and even vulnerable to the way *life* tests him and tries his values. Such a man does not take his values for granted and is responsible for his moral convictions; they are not just something given, part of his childhood cargo as I put it earlier. His love or regard for them has been tried, and so *he* has been tried. We could say that his love has been transformed from a passive habit to an active attitude of will.

This maturity in a person's relation to the values in which he believes is part of the maturity that characterizes his relation to himself as this appears in the way he lives, responds to things, carries out his undertakings, and cares for others. We may describe him as true to himself and as acting on his own behalf. I believe these, namely *authenticity* and *autonomy*, to be the key notions in terms of which self-knowledge is to be understood. The knowledge in question, as I said before, characterizes the way the person is, and not his beliefs about himself. A person who lacks it is one who is either emotionally immature or deceived in himself. He lacks self-criticism, self-control and self-reliance, or the kind of respect for others which acknowledges their independent existence.[2] We can say that he does not know who he is or where he stands.

I have argued that this is not the same thing as not knowing 'what one is like', although one would hardly expect a person who doesn't know that to have self-knowledge. Thus while Freud is right to insist that 'making the unconscious conscious' is the pivot around which psycho-analytic therapy revolves, he sometimes gives the impression that this is *all* that coming to know oneself consists of. He recognizes that this is bound to be puzzling: 'You imagined the recovery of a nervous person rather differently, that after he had been subjected to the laborious process of psycho-analysis he would emerge a different person altogether, and then you hear that the whole thing amounts to his having a little less that is unconscious and a little more that is conscious in him than before' (1949a, p. 363).

Freud is right in thinking that our puzzlement springs, partly, from our failure to appreciate the character and importance of such a change. We fail to recognize how much this involves the giving up of defensive postures and the recognition of new possibilities. It opens up for the analysand ways that were blocked to him and frees his vitality so that

---

[2] Without such respect he cannot find himself in his relationships with other people, he cannot learn from and grow in his interaction with them.

he can put it into creative ventures. It provides him with an opportunity to find what he wants and to make something of himself, to grow out of old modes of relationship and develop in new ones. While some of these changes constitute the 'enlargement of consciousness' we discussed earlier (chapter 4, section 4) they also go beyond it. Freud recognized this when later he described the aim of psycho-analytic therapy in terms of the 'enlargement of the self' — not simply in terms of the enlargement of what the self knows about itself: 'Where id is there ego shall be.' He also talked of a reduction in the severity of the super-ego. He could have put this as: 'Where super-ego is there ego shall be.'[3] It is clear that what is in question is the development of the ego, and not simply the enlargement of its consciousness. This involves the will. It means that the analysand is no longer subject to impulsive or compulsive action, over-concerned with pleasing others, doing things in order to be accepted, or acting defiantly when hopeless about achieving acceptability. What counts for him now is what *he* thinks is right. He takes responsibility for what he does — he stands by it, is prepared to justify it when challenged, and if things go wrong he does not shun blame, accepts punishment, and is willing to pay for his mistakes. This is the mark of autonomy.

This is knowledge of the self insofar as being a self means being oneself, endorsing one's deepest beliefs, shouldering responsibility for what one does. A man who doesn't know what he wants does not have a self to know. All he knows are the impulses and inclinations he is subject to, or what other people expect or think of him. A man who doesn't know where he stands does not have a mind of his own to make up. He can, therefore, only yield to impulse or conform to something outside himself. In either case he lacks authenticity. Psycho-analysis forces him to become responsible for what he is. It faces him with his innermost conflicts and the need to make up his mind. It does not merely get him to recognize something already in existence, i.e. his unconscious emotions and inclinations; it also faces him with his evasions, i.e. the

---

[3] Melanie Klein speaks of the super-ego's gradual transformation into conscience in the true sense of the word. See Klein (1948), p. 68.

decisions and stands he has *not* taken. It is in this way that it forces him to decide: to take charge of inclinations he has avoided recognizing, to make them his own and build on them or to give them up. This is the way that psycho-analysis engages the will and promotes self-knowledge. So long as the analysand remains passive the analysis cannot progress. And insofar as he lacks what would make for growth and constructiveness it cannot succeed.

Coming to self-knowledge is thus finding oneself, although as we have seen this is not something within one waiting to be discovered. The inward journey in analysis faces the analysand with what he has turned away from and left undone. The less he has to evade, the more he can turn outwards. It is there, in what he takes an interest in and gives himself to, that he finds himself. For 'finding' here means making something of oneself. This involves moral and emotional growth which, in turn, presupposes interaction with one's social environment at every level — acquiring new ideas and forms of thought, assimilating new values, modes of criticism and perception, entering into new activities, finding new interests, and forming new relationships, while in all this remaining one's own man.

It has been thought by some that in focusing the analysand's attention on himself psycho-analysis is bound to promote self-absorption: 'Too much attention to facts about oneself may lead, not to self-knowledge . . . but to self-consciousness' (Hamlyn, 1977, p. 174). 'Forgetfulness of self has long been regarded as essential to virtue and sanity. On the psychiatrist's couch it is remembrance of self that is demanded.'[4] This is the reverse of the truth. Insofar as psycho-analysis helps the analysand to give up his defences it will leave him a prey to the infantile dependence and narcissism which his mature exterior masks; or at any rate he will be exposed to the temptation to regress to these early modes of relationship. To the extent to which he is narcissistic his thoughts and associations will turn inwards and linger there caressingly. To the extent to which he is masochistic he will dwell on his

---

[4] From a review in *The Listener* of Ernest Jones' biography of Freud — date *circa* 1961.

faults and failures, criticizing himself with some pleasure and turning this into a substitute for change. To the extent to which he has made an idealized past into a haven from his difficulties in growing up he will take refuge in it, in his dreams and associations he will keep returning to that time. These different forms of self-absorption may be said to be promoted by analysis insofar as they are the result of the removal of the analysand's defences and of a setting that encourages regression. But they are themselves *resistances* to the progress of analysis towards greater self-knowledge. So the task of analysis is to help the analysand to dispense with them too, to reverse the trends which they represent. It will succeed, if it can find in the analysand a will to grow up and venture forth[5] and make contact with it, if it can help him to see in the light of the present those dangers which in the past frightened him into postures of dependence and security. For the rest this will to venture forth will find nourishment in his outside interests. Such a change in the analysand will find expression in his associations, in his relationship with the analyst, and in what he makes of the analysis. In this way focusing attention on himself will eventually lead the analysand away from self-absorption and towards greater self-knowledge in the sense I have tried to elucidate.

[5] H. and B. Overstreet refer to this as 'restorative power', 'emotional resilience' and 'comeback power' without further analysis. See Overstreet and Overstreet, 1954, chapter 1.

9

Determinism and Order in the Human Mind

1 Determinism and Causality

It seemed to Freud a philosophical prejudice to think that man's life and behaviour may not be subject to causality: 'Are you asking me, gentlemen, to believe that there is anything which happens without a cause?' He believed that to think so is to throw over 'the whole scientific outlook on the world' (1949a, p. 21). To think of mental phenomena as failing to come 'within the causal sequence of things', he thought, is to turn them into arbitrary, accidental, random, unpredictable events, unrelated to their subject's character, his past life and present circumstances. So he speaks of 'the thorough-going meaningfulness and determinism of even the apparently most obscure and arbitrary mental phenomena' (see Jones, 1954, p. 401).

Freud further thought that determinism, in this sense, once embraced has the consequence of denying the freedom of the will: 'There is within you a deeply rooted belief in psychic freedom and choice, . . . this belief is quite unscientific, and . . . it must give ground before the claims of a determinism which governs even mental life' (1949a, pp. 87–8). Insofar as this belief does involve confusion Freud is right in wishing to reject it. But the trouble is that he is himself confused. So before we can appreciate Freud's positive contribution here we must examine the confusion in question.

It has been pointed out that 'though caused an act may be free — as long as it is not compelled'. There is something right about this claim; but it does not go to the root of the trouble. A river may be said to run freely if there is no obstruction that dams its flow, a wheel may be said to turn freely if there is no friction to slow it down — in contrast, for instance, with a bicycle wheel, slightly out of alignment, so that it rubs against the brake. In other words, although the movement of the river and the wheel are causally determined they may still be free. With human actions it is the same. Just as when we give a causal explanation of the downhill flow of the river we do not imply that its flow is not free, so too when we give an explanation of a man's action and say, for instance, that he left his wife because he was fed up with her constant nagging, we do not imply that he did not act freely.

Still, as Wisdom points out, there is all the difference between the movement of a wheel or the flow of a river and the actions of a human being: 'We think of a human being who runs to help another as acting freely, as having been free to do something different, in a way in which a machine doesn't act freely however freely it runs. Surely we think of human beings as having a freedom which machines have not' (1965, p. 26). Wisdom here is drawing attention to a difference in grammar, for it has to do with such facts as that we can speak of a man's movement as being voluntary or involuntary, describe human beings as taking decisions, forming intensions, keeping promises, thinking and deliberating before they act, wanting things, searching for ways of satisfying their desires, holding them in check, and so on. Whereas it makes no sense to speak of a river or a wheel in these terms.

We do not account for a man's actions and decisions in the way that we account for physical phenomena. But this does not mean that we do not account for human actions and decisions, nor that we do not make predictions about what men will do and the outcome of their deliberations. For instance, if you know a man well you can sometimes predict what sorts of reason and consideration will weigh with him in particular circumstances, and so you can tell what he will do or how he will act. One may characterize such predictions as 'vague', but this is not to find fault with them. It isn't like saying of a particular prediction in astronomy that it is vague. For there we are contrasting it with the sort of prediction that ought to be made or aimed at. And, of course, that one can explain why a man decided as he did, or that one can predict his decisions in some circumstances, in no way shows that his decisions are unfree.

Where we are concerned with causes we can predict an event from its causal antecedents. But this does not make the event inevitable or unavoidable. When we make such a prediction it is not part of what we claim that the event we predict is unavoidable. If we say that an event will occur, say an explosion or a war, and *add* that it is unavoidable, we are suggesting that we have no means of preventing it, or that those who have the means will do nothing to prevent it. For instance, death was unavoidable at one time for those who had severe tuberculosis; but this is no longer so. This is just as true of the predictions we make in connection with human actions, even though these predictions are of a different kind. For instance, knowing a man's political convictions, his courage, and the issues at stake in the coming elections I may be able to predict how he will vote. There is no suggestion that it is inevitable that he should vote this way.

It is true that this is not typical of most situations in which men make decisions and act. For often the issues are complex and not clear cut. Besides, in many situations, what the alternatives are, what a man can do, depends to some extent on how imaginative he is. And we cannot take this into account in what we predict in the way we take his convictions and his courage into account. For one thing, knowing that he is imaginative will not help us much unless we are as imaginative ourselves. In any case, the predictions we make can only be vague. In most cases we can at best predict the *kind* of thing he will do, or that he will *not* do certain things which others in a similar situation may do. As for what a man will say in conversation, what we can predict here is pretty limited; which is not to say that much of what a man says in conversation is random. What we can predict here is fixed by what it means to carry on a conversation and the way a conservation differs from a drill, ceremony or game, and by what it is possible for a man to bring to a conversation. I think that this is to a large extent true of a large area of human actions as well.

Prediction of human actions and decisions, then, has a special character which calls for further reflection. But where it is possible to predict a man's actions and decisions this does not mean that they are not free. Nor, where it is not possible to predict them, does this mean that they are random or haphazard.

I said that we do not account for a man's actions and decisions in terms of causes. But what reasons weigh with a man, the way he thinks about various matters, the kinds of thing that attract him, depend on his upbringing and his previous experiences. So can we not say that they determine his actions and the way he chooses? And if so, is it not true that they make it impossible for him to act and choose differently from the way he does? In that case, can he be said to have any freedom of action and choice? Any say in what he does?

One needs to be careful here; but I shall be brief. A man is what he is because of what has happened to him, because of what he has met in life, and also because of what he has made of it. It would be a gross over-simplification to think of this 'determination' or 'formation' on the analogy of the completion of a manufactured product — even if in certain extreme cases it may come near to it. Thus think of Aldous Huxley's 'Brave New World'. A man's tastes, inclinations and moral beliefs are formed through a period of evolution the course of which is subject to a great many influences. But this does not mean that he is simply a 'product' of these in the sense that it is not he who determines what he wants, that he does not act on his own behalf. Certainly to be able to choose and act at all a man has to have certain tastes, beliefs, inclinations, interests. Without them he does not have a soul to call his own or a mind to make up. It is in the light of these that he takes decisions and acts in particular situations. It is what interferes with his doing so that restricts his freedom. But his beliefs and inclinations, and what has contributed to their formation, cannot be said to do so. Again, he could be described as not being a free agent, as being subject to outside influences, if his tastes and inclinations were not his own, if for instance he were subservient to public opinion, a follower of cults and fads. But the fact that what is outside him has contributed to their development, that he is what he is as a result of what he has learnt in his interaction with others in the context of a life which exists independently of him, does not mean that he is 'alienated' from what makes him the way he is.

'What has gone to make him the way he is makes it impossible for him to act and choose differently from the way he does.' This makes it seem as if he is impotent, as if it is an illusion that he acts, as if his actions are determined not by him but by something outside him. But I have suggested that 'what has gone to make him' does not curtail his powers of action, it creates the possibility of their exercise. Perhaps one is trying to say that what has gone to make him the way he is makes it impossible for him to *want* to act and choose differently from the way he does. But this only means that he acts as an agent with a mind and a will of his own. If so, there is no implication that what has gone to make him the way he is curtails his freedom. For that freedom is the freedom to act as he *wants* to — he is free if his actions come from *him*. However the expression 'make it impossible' makes it seem as if he has been twisted to want to act in the way he wants to act. And while that could be true in particular cases, there is no reason to think that it must be so in every case. I have suggested that the fact that a man owes his being to what exists independently of him is no good reason for thinking so. What a man wants is not something that is simply *given*. It is something to the formation of which he enters reflectively, something which he can search for and make up his mind to and, therefore, something which involves his responsibility.

This search, however, does not take place in a vacuum, in a limitless space, so to speak. And although what is signalled by the use of such expressions as 'he now knows what he wants' involves an extension of the self, it also implies the existence of something like a hard core which permits such an extension. Not everything that a person can imagine and wish for constitutes a genuine possibility for him. Many writers, psychoanalytic and otherwise, have pointed this out: 'She [Kitty] had deceived herself in supposing that she could be what she wanted to be' (Tolstoy, 1956, p. 256). 'No man becomes this or that by wishing to be it, however earnestly' (Schopenhauer, 1951, part vi, p. 52). 'The psyche has, one might almost say, a kind of solid substantiality of its own which we cannot alter at will, and which we have to begin by accepting and respecting. Thus, we cannot ourselves, by wishful thinking, become anything we would like to be, we cannot by an effort of will make ourselves *feel* differently from the ways in which we discover that we do feel. We do not choose what we shall feel . . . At any moment we are what we are, and we can become different only by slow processes of growth . . . Our conscious mental operations do not convey the full force of this stubborn durability of psychic reality, since it is relatively easy to change our ideas, to alter our decisions, to vary our pursuits and interests, and so on; but we can do all that without becoming very different basically as persons' (Guntrip, 1977, p. 218). This point is well illustrated in Tolstoy's description of Father Sergius' struggles with himself to live up to his ideals (see Tolstoy, 1960).

Someone who has reflected on the point being made may say: 'There are limits to a person's freedom, though these limits can be extended.' I feel uneasy about putting it this way; it seems to me that there is a whole spectrum of cases here which need distinguishing from each other. The limits that a man comes up against in some of these are not limits to his freedom. This needs discussion. The reason I mention it now is because when Freud and some of the early psychoanalysts took determinism to be a denial of free will, they were equating a 'belief in free will' with a belief in an unrelated spontaneity' (Jones, 1974, p. 186). As Brill put it: Men cannot 'do what they want regardless of motives and according to their free will' (1948, p. 87). So Freud thinks that where a man believes he has no reason or motive for doing what he does he will think that he is acting in accordance with his own free will: the 'conviction that there is a free will . . . does not manifest itself in weighty and important decisions' (1954b, p. 212). 'Man's belief in free will seems to be stronger in proportion to the unimportance of the decision. Everyone is convinced that he is free to choose whether to stand or sit at a given moment, to cross his right leg over his left or *vice versa* "as he wishes'" (Jones, 1974, pp. 181—2). Freud then argues that even in these cases we do not act of our own free will: 'It is impossible to think of a number, or even of a name, of one's own free will' (1954b, p. 193).

Freud's and Jones's idea of free will is fairly widespread and involves at least two confusions: the confusion of 'reason' with 'cause', and of 'cause' with 'compulsion'. André Gide caricatured this idea in his novel *Les Caves du Vatican* where the hero Lafcadio pushes a complete stranger out of a train in order to prove that he is free. As Sartre pointed out, this so-called 'gratuitous act' is an act of pure caprice (1970, p. 48). As such it is not a free action; nor is it one that cannot be explained in terms of the agent's beliefs, ideas, phantasies, motives and intentions. Often a person acts capriciously because he feels he must affirm his independence, and he feels this because he feels his independence to be shaky. In his capricious acts he thus acts in slavery to a misguided desire to be extravagant, original, independent or free. But he cannot become independent in this way, nor can he achieve an original action — one that comes from him. Hence Guntrip's point that we cannot become anything we would like to be — by wishful thinking or an effort of will. We can only become different by a slow process of growth. This takes patience and application, respect for the way we are rather than running away from it. Lafcadio's 'gratuitous act' is, therefore, a form of self-evasion.

What a person is up against in these many cases is the resilience of the self, the limits and limitations of formed character. But it is a mistake to think that they are propped up by a chain of causes. As for the exercise of free will, this is something that takes place within these limits.

2   Causal Necessity

I claimed that Freud's determinsim partly comes from his commitment to the law of causality. I also said that in his mind there is a confusion between 'reason', 'cause' and 'compulsion'. As we shall see there is something sound in what he was putting forward in the name of determinism, namely the 'meaningfulness of even the apparently most obscure and arbitrary mental phenomena'. But he was wrong to think of this as the extension of the law of causality to the sphere of the human mind. We shall also see that although he was wrong to think that his brand of determinism entailed the denial of human freedom, nevertheless this denial was the expression of a vision of the state in which men, as a matter of fact, find themselves. But before we can appreciate these two points we have further ground to cover. As part of this I want to raise two questions: Does one have to accept the law of causality in the sphere of the mind? And if one did, what would follow from this acceptance? I shall consider these questions in the reverse order.

Moore who, like Freud, accepted the law of causality, argued that nothing follows from it that puts our belief in the freedom of the will at jeopardy. In chapter 6 of his book *Ethics* he examines an argument for the view that free will is an illusion. This conclusion is derived from the premise that everything that happens has a cause, or is caused by something that preceded it. Does the premise entail that what happens, in any particular case, was *bound* to happen, so that nothing else could have happened instead? Moore thinks that there is a sense of the word 'could' in which this does follow, but that in *that* sense the conclusion does not exclude the reality of free will. When we say that we have free will all that we mean is that we *could* have done things, which in fact we did not do, had we chosen to do them. But this sense of 'could' is not the same as the sense of the word 'could' in the conclusion which does follow from the premise that everything that happens has a cause. Hence our belief in the freedom of the will is not incompatible with the law of causality.

What is the sense of 'could' in which it is certain that we often *could* have done what we did not do? Moore's answer is that in this sense, 'I could have done otherwise', means, 'I would have done otherwise *if* I had chosen to'. But from the law of causality it does *not* follow that I could do no other than what I did, even if I had chosen to do otherwise. Determination by antecedent causes does not exclude this.

Moore is certain that there is a sense in which we often *can* do what we in fact do not do. This is the sense of 'can' in terms of which we distinguish between the man in whose power it is to do something he envisages doing and the man in whose power it is not to do so. As he puts it: 'No distinction is commoner than this' (1947, p. 127). In other words, Moore is reminding us of a distinction we often make and, therefore, find intelligible. He is reminding us of a sense of 'can' in which the word is applicable to human actions. He reminds us of it because it is precisely what is denied by the determinist who thinks, mistakenly, that 'everything has a cause' entails that 'nothing ever could have happened except what did happen', so that whatever we do we could not have done otherwise.

According to Moore what the determinist denies is that this distinction which we commonly make between some human actions and others *makes sense*. He denies it because he is misled by an ambiguity in the sense of the words 'can' and 'could'. What is the distinction and the sense of 'can' or 'could' relevant to it? Moore answers: 'Only a few instances need be given. I *could* have walked a mile in twenty minutes this morning, but I certainly could *not* have run two miles in five minutes. I did not, *in fact*, do either of these two things, but it is pure nonsense to say that the mere fact that I *did not, does away* with the distinction between them, which I express by saying that the one *was* within my powers, whereas the other was *not*. *Although* I did neither, yet the one was certainly *possible* to me in the sense in which the other was totally *im*possible' (1947, p. 128). He goes on: 'Instances of this sort might be multiplied quite indefinitely; and it is surely quite plain that we all of us do *continually* use such language: we continually, when considering two events, neither of which *did* happen, distinguish between them by saying that whereas the one *was* possible, though it didn't happen, the other was *im*possible.' He concludes: 'It is, therefore, quite certain that we often *could* (in *some* sense) have done what we did not do' (p. 129). This is obviously a *grammatical* conclusion and Moore supports it by reminding us of the way we talk.

The determinist claims: 'Whatever we do we could not have done otherwise; it was necessarily inevitable that we should do it.' Moore denies this claim. It makes perfectly good sense to say such things as, 'If I want to, I can do it', 'If I choose to, I can leave you', 'If I had wanted to I could have slapped you on the face, but I chose not to'. There are occasions when a man says such a thing and in saying it speaks truly. So if what I do not in fact do is within my power to do, then it is not because it is impossible for me to do it that I don't do it. Nothing need prevent me from doing it, I may simply choose not to do it. Conversely, there is nothing inevitable about what I do do, I may do it because it is what I want to do and have decided to do it.

Moore is certain that we have free will. It turns out that this amounts to claiming that it *makes sense* to speak in certain ways about human actions and, therefore, in speaking in these ways sometimes speak truly. He concludes that whatever follows from the law of causality it cannot be anything which contradicts this. The determinist thinks that it does. Therefore he must be wrong. What makes this mistake possible is an ambiguity in the words 'can' and 'could' which the determinist overlooks. However, as far as I can see, Moore does not make clear the other sense of 'could' in which it does really follow from the law of causality that 'nothing ever *could* have happened, except what did happen' (p. 130).

I think that the argument (see Moore, 1947, p. 129) in which this conclusion is derived from the law of causality is suspect and the conclusion is completely empty. Converting the conclusion we get: whatever happens is *inevitable* – or was *bound* to happen. The reason given for it is that it has a cause. But does a cause make what it brings about inevitable? Can we not arrange for the cause to be realized *without* the effect we would normally expect being realized? We can. For instance, someone has set up the charges with which he intends to blow up a bridge. Pressing the button before him will bring this about. I cut the wire or disconnect the charges, as a result of which what would bring about the explosion fails to do so and the blowing up of the bridge is averted. Someone may object that what I allow to take place is not the cause of what has been averted; it *could not* have been. For though a necessary condition for the realization of what has been averted, it was not a sufficient condition. If it were both necessary and sufficient, then the bridge would have been blown up inevitably, and nothing could have averted it once those conditions were realized.

But is this the way we use the term 'cause'? I think not. For by 'cause' we usually mean what would bring about something fairly specific in certain conditions. There is no implication that if what we call 'the cause' does take place in those circumstances then the effect *must* take place — *necessarily*. For however fully one specifies the causal antecedents or conditions, one can never exclude something *further* happening, something that one can arrange to happen, so that what would otherwise have taken place does not do so. This cannot be logically excluded.[1] In other words, in principle, whatever can be predicted on causal grounds can be averted. A causal prediction does not claim that something will happen inevitably. Of course, we may not in a particular case have the knowledge to be able to avert what we expect to happen. In such a case we say that what we expect to happen is inevitable. But, as I said before, this is an additional claim; it says that we are impotent or unwilling to avert it.

To sharpen the distinction one could say that there are two senses of 'inevitable' — 'absolutely inevitable' and 'relatively inevitable'. Absolute inevitability means logical necessity, and this is a chimera where causes or causal chains are concerned. Here there is room only for *relative inevitability*, that is inevitability relative to our knowledge, our interest and willingness to do something about what is expected or anticipated. This, I believe, is the sense on which Moore focused in his phrase, 'I could, if I chose to'. Thus the ambiguity which Moore claims for the words 'can' and 'could' is between relative and absolute possibility, i.e. between material and logical possibility. But in that case, what is the sense of 'could' in which, according to Moore, the conclusion, 'Nothing ever could have happened except what did happen' does really follow from the law of causality? Not 'could not' in the sense of 'relatively impossible'. Moore is right on this point. But neither is it 'could not' in the sense of 'absolutely impossible'. There is, indeed, *no* sense of 'could not' in which the above conclusion follows from the law of causality.

---

[1] I have discussed this question in detail in Dilman, 1973a, chapter 10, 'Logical Connections and Causal Ties'.

To say of a particular action that it was relatively inevitable, i.e. that he could not have done otherwise even if he had wanted and chosen to do otherwise, is to make a *factual claim* about the action and the agent. It is to say that he is not free or that he is weak-willed. If true, it must be possible for this to be false. We cannot apply it indiscriminately to all human beings or all human actions; and neither can such a claim be deduced from the law of causality.

But what does the law of causality claim anyway? And why should we adhere to it in connection with human agency and the mind? In the *Tractatus* Wittgenstein said that 'the law of causality is not a law but the form of a law' (1961, 6.32). He said further that 'what the law of causality is meant to exclude cannot even be described' (6.362). To appreciate Wittgenstein's point let us contrast the law of causality with a genuine causal hypothesis — say, that there is a causal connection between smoking and lung cancer. What is this hypothesis meant to exclude? Roughly: many instances of people smoking regularly without contracting lung cancer. The particular case that conflicts with the hypothesis is no threat to it. For, quite apart from the statistical character of what it claims, we may discover special features in the conflicting cases which account for the non-occurrence of lung cancer — e.g. metabolic processes which reduce or neutralize the tars deposited in the smoker's lungs.

What about the law of causality itself: what does it exclude? For instance, that lung cancer may have no cause? What does that mean? Of course, nobody may know for sure *what* causes lung cancer, and there was presumably a time when faced with such a disease scientists had no idea where to begin their investigation and what to investigate. Presumably, as they studied particular cases, compared and contrasted them, developed criteria of identification and so began to form a particular conception of the disease, ideas of how its causes are to be investigated began to emerge. Such a development, presumably, took place side by side with many other similar developments in other areas of human knowledge and within the very broad framework of a general pattern — the pattern of causal inquiry.

That a particular disease, such as lung cancer, may not have a cause is now unthinkable. That lung cancer may have no cause is not an hypothesis open to investigation. For what would an investigation be here but a causal one! Our very notion of disease, whether it be lung cancer or measles, brings in the idea of a causal investigation, so that particular diseases of the kind raise causal questions for us. And a causal investigation is undertaken to find out *what* are the causes of a particular phenomenon; *not* to find out *whether* such phenomena have a cause. As Rhees once put it: ' "Some things happen without causes" is shocking when it is said in connection with causal inquiry, because it seems to be a statement in the grammar of causal investigation.'

What about indeterminacy in quantum physics? This is a big question to which the short answer is that certain facts in a particular area of scientific investigation may make it pointless for scientists to stick to methods that have served them well elsewhere. As Wittgenstein puts it: 'Certain events would put me into a position in which I could not go on with the old language-game any further' (1969b, section 617). By 'could not' he means 'would not want to', 'would not see any point in'.

I asked what it means to reject the possibility of uncaused events in macro-physics. I pointed out that within the framework of the kind of investigation we carry out here such a possibility is ruled out for us, it makes no sense. Its making no sense is bound up with the kinds of concept in terms of which we think *here*. I only mentioned the concept of a disease like lung cancer. But elsewhere, where we speak in a different grammar, use different concepts, causal questions may not arise, or fade into the background. Freud asked rhetorically whether he was supposed 'to believe that there is anything which happens without a cause'. Nevertheless the account he gave of human behaviour, except sometimes in appearance, was far from being a causal account: 'By abandoning a part of our psychic capacity as unexplainable through *purposive ideas* we ignore the realm of determinism in our mental life' (1954b, p. 193 — italics mine). From the very beginning when Freud talked of 'the existence of an interplay of forces' he meant 'the operation of intentions and purposes such as are to be observed in normal life' (1948b, p. 40). Thus in rejecting the possibility that any 'mental occurrence' should 'fail to come within the causal sequence of things' (1949a, p. 21), he was in reality rejecting the possibility of actions and reactions that do not make sense in terms of the agent's or patient's character, motives, intentions, thoughts and emotions — conscious and unconscious. And in doing so he was not advancing a very general hypothesis about mental life. He was trying to develop a general framework or grammar for psychological investigation, especially into mental disturbances and abnormalities of various kinds.[2]

Freud did indeed extend the sphere of determinism to cover mental life. But in doing so he inevitably transformed it. We could say that his determinism is related to physical determinism, except that it is in a different grammar. It is not a determinism of causes, but one of intentions and ideas. And just as physical determinism does not exclude the possibility of men changing and controlling the course of those physical events which affect their lives, so similarly mental determinism, in the sense under consideration, does not exclude the possibility of free will and self-determination.

3   'The Meaningfulness of Mental Phenomena'

I said that Freud's determinism is an attempt to develop a very general framework for psychological investigation. The vision behind this program is in many ways like the vision of great novelists in whose writings both the most ordinary actions and the craziest are seen to bear the stamp of their characters' individuality and to assume a new dimension of sense in the context of their lives. The framework Freud tried to work out for such a vision bears this broad resemblance to the law of causality which, as I pointed out, belongs to the framework of the physical science. It enables us to see order in and make sense of phenomena which otherwise would seem haphazard and arbitrary, even though the terms of reference in which the ordering is carried out are very different and 'sense' does not mean the same thing in the two connections.

---

[2] Here too we have a conceptual innovation. Compare with what I said about Freud's 'discovery' of the unconscious.

However, Freud was misled in working out the details of the framework for his vision — for instance, when he suggested that all dreams are the expression of imaginary wish fulfilments, that all failures of memory are instances of repression, that all slips of the tongue are to be explained in the same way.[3] In this he gave way to a craving for generality which I do not think his determinism demanded. For there is a big difference between saying that all the actions and reactions of a person, even those that seem the most senseless and arbitrary, must bear *some* relation to his life and character, and saying that they must bear *the same kind* of relation to these. I think that Freud's determinism gets into trouble when it assumes that there is one fundamental type of relation, that ultimately all human actions and reactions are related to the agent's or patient's character *in the same way*.

Take the case of forgetting or slips of the tongue, for instance. As a matter of fact we have different ways of accounting for such phenomena. We distinguish between genuinely forgetting, which admits of degrees, and being unable to recollect, although one has not really forgotten. Freud could not really have wanted to say that we never forget anything, though he was at times carried away in this direction. The important thing for a psycho-analyst, surely, is to be able to identify correctly instances where a person's inability to recollect something is not a genuine loss of memory. Here Freud showed genius, and he was right to emphasize that such cases are more common than we think. Similarly for what we call 'accidents' — a man knocking down and smashing an expensive vase for instance. It would be absurd to think that no man can knock down a piece of furniture or hurt himself when hammering a nail accidentally, without it being his intention to do so. Here too a psycho-analyst has to be able to sort out, in particular cases, what is a genuine accident from what is only apparently so. Freud's

---

[3] Compare with the tendency to think that *all* moral attitudes are defensive measures, *all* mourning is a working through of one's ambivalence towards a loved person one has lost, *all* love is a transference phenomenon, *all* men are self-seeking and pleasure-loving. Freud should have known better than to think so, although these tendencies and pulls are in his thinking.

contribution was to draw attention to affinities between *some* instances where a man cuts his hand or knocks down a vase apparently by accident and others where he enjoys doing so, where he seeks to punish himself, to communicate something, in short, where his doing so is part of his design. For instance, his clumsy acts may be an attempt to appear helpless and draw attention to himself.

Obviously, if a person knocks down a vase by accident this will not bear any relation to his life and character. But if it is a genuine accident can we describe what is in question as an action or reaction? By a reaction I mean something like slapping someone on the face in anger, bursting into tears on hearing a distressing piece of news, twitching nervously while waiting for an interview, becoming confused, one's mind going black, forgetting one's lines, just where one wants to succeed or make a good impression. It is in instances of the latter kind that Freud is not content to rest with such answers as 'His mind went blank because he was nervous, and he was nervous because so much was at stake for him.' This may well be true, of course, and the connection in question perfectly intelligible. Still Freud believes that there is room for probing here, a probing in the direction of something more distinctively personal. But need there be some further explanation in *every* case? Should we never take a statement like the above as the final explanation? Freud's answer in connection with slips and errors was this: 'We do not maintain – and for our purposes we do not need to maintain – that every single mistake which occurs has a meaning, although I think that probable. It is enough for us to prove that such a meaning is relatively frequent in the various forms of errors. (1949a, p. 47).

Freud explains that by 'meaning' he understands 'significance, intention, tendency and a position in the sequence of mental concatenations' (1949a, p. 48). Thus when, for instance, the word which a person intended to speak enables a different word to escape him, or when he inadvertently distorts it so that what comes out of his mouth is related to a different word, the word uttered or suggested may express a thought or an affective response which he was checking, though he was not aware of it. Compare with the case where the words which a person speaks in anger may reveal what he really thinks. He may himself be surprised and when he reverts to his everyday slightly deferential attitude, he may dismiss his words as a 'lapse': 'Those words were spoken in anger, they do not reflect what I think of you.' Compare with: 'That was not him; it was the alcohol speaking.'

Freud's view is that there is a variety of instances in which the truth, in the sense of what a person really thinks or feels, his real reactions or preoccupations, escapes him in unguarded moments, in moments when his powers of attention and self-control are low. It escapes him in words, errors, inadvertent acts, and omissions which may look innocent, so that we are tempted to take them at face value and dismiss them as 'insignificant' or 'trivial'. We do so because there is no conscious intention on the part of the person in question, because it does not fit in with his conscious thoughts and deliberate actions. Freud's view is that if we can take a more intimate and comprehensive view of the person, and this would involve a willingness on his part to be conversationally open with us, then we may find that it does fit in. This may change the aspect under which we see it. Such a change of aspect *for him* involves taking responsibility for certain thoughts and attitudes which, previously, he had been unwilling to own.

Freud is critical of this kind of dismissiveness: 'Here, as in still other spheres, determinism reaches farther than we suppose' (1954b, p. 193). In the previous sentence he makes it clear that an act which seems arbitrary, in the way that an error is arbitrary, is subject to determinism if it is 'explainable through purposive ideas'. 'That there should be uncaused events is unthinkable.' I commented on this earlier. 'That there should be innocent slips, errors or omissions, purely accidental acts, is unthinkable.' Freud is inclined to go that way, but he restrains himself, and rightly so: fewer of them are innocent than we suppose. Perhaps his view is that in psycho-analysis we should not assume them innocent until they are proven otherwise, that we should start with the reverse assumption and hold on to it until we have been proven wrong. Perhaps this is the sense of his words: 'determinism reaches farther than we suppose'.

When Freud spoke of 'determinism' and 'the meaningfulness of mental phenomena' he did not only mention the parapraxes which he discusses in *Psychopathology of Everyday Life*, but also dreams and neurotic symptoms. Each of these raise new difficulties. In my few comments I shall confine myself to the case of dreams. In *The Interpretation of Dreams* Freud argues that dreams are a form of thought, in some ways akin to daydreams and in others to hallucinations. They are also, often, a form of memory, in the way in which Proust's 'affective memories' are a form of memory: 'In the dream we knew and remembered something which was beyond the reach of our waking memory' (1967, p. 45). So he describes dreams as 'products of our own mental activity' (p. 80). 'Every dream reveals itself as a psychical structure which has a meaning and which can be inserted at an assignable point in the mental activities of waking life' (p. 35). To assign a 'meaning' to a dream is 'replacing it by something which fits into the chain of our mental acts as a link having a validity and importance equal to the rest' (p. 128). The parallel with what he says about the 'meaning' of slips, omissions and symptomatic acts is clear. In his *Introductory Lectures* he says that 'dreams are not a somatic, but a mental, phenomenon' (1949a, p. 82) and he speaks of them as 'the life of the mind during sleep' (p. 71).

'Not a somatic phenomenon': Freud means that the dream is not an epiphenomenon or 'froth'. In other words, the dreamer's mind finds expression in his dreams, the dreams are the form which his mental activities and passivities, his thoughts and emotions, take while he is asleep. But this raises philosophical difficulties. Can we attribute thoughts and emotions to a sleeper? If not, then although the patient's dream reports can still be subjected to interpretation, on a par with the phantasies which he puts into words, we cannot speak of dreams as 'the life of the mind during sleep'. I have argued elsewhere that these difficulties are not insuperable and that there is no objection to thinking of dreams as the vehicle through which the sleeper's mental life finds expression (see Dilman, 1966), and I will not here repeat the arguments I put forward for this view.

One parallel between dreams and parapraxes is this. In both cases what we have is not subject to the conscious will and what finds expression is outside the province of the person's vigilance. This is what makes it of value to the psycho-analyst. Freud's thesis is that in these two phenomena we have what seems most remote from *psychological* interpreta-tion; yet they can be treated as among the most expressive of just those preoccupations and responses that are kept at bay in a person's deliberate thoughts and actions. Thus Freud talks of dreams as 'the royal road to a knowledge of the uncon-scious' (1967, p. 647) — provided one knows how to interpret them. This raises the question of the justification of treating them in this way and of the criteria for the truth of the interpretations put forward. I postpone a discussion of the second question until my study of psycho-analytic therapy, *Insight and Therapy* (see Introduction above). As for the justification of treating dreams as an expression of the uncon-scious mind, this is clearly bound up with Freud's thesis that the less vigilant a person is, the more off his guard he is, the more are the acts, words, thoughts and responses that come from him expressive of those emotions and preoccupations which are excluded from those activities in which his actions are responsible to public norms. But how is this thesis to be substantiated? I think by a selection of examples which give credibility to it and by reflecting on these examples. Sub-stantiation here takes the form of illustration; and this is, of course, how novelists often open our eyes to a general truth we have failed to recognize.

The truth in question in this case may be approached by reflecting on the following kind of consideration. Take the case of a sergeant major giving orders to the men he is training. Since this is what one would expect any sergeant major to do there is nothing particularly significant in his doing what he does. On the other hand, something of his sarcasm, or his anxiety to be always on top, or the pleasure he gets in impos-ing his will on others, or the insecurity he tries to deal with in controlling the men in his charge, may betray itself in the way he gives orders. Of course, we shall know what to make of these expressions the more we come to know him, and that means the greater our acquaintance with other aspects of his life. The light which these throw on each other is mutual. But this is not my point at the moment. What finds expression in the manner in which he conducts his work will become bolder or plainer the more he is at home in this work, the more liberties he takes with the men during the course of a drill. And the plainer still when he mixes with the men during a break: in the way he jokes with them, or exploits his position of superiority. He is no longer acting simply as a sergeant major, but as a person who spreads his inner life into this outer role.

I am not saying, of course, that a person cannot put himself into his work; that would be absurd. A man who can do so will, in fact, find himself in his work. Insofar as he can do so he will succeed in resolving his inner conflicts in the context of his work. On the other hand, insofar as he is unable to do so there will be aspects of his inner life to which this work will remain alien. It is these that I was referring to when I spoke of him as spreading them into the carrying out of that work. Doing so is bringing something external into that work. That is why it is by taking liberties with what that work requires of him that these aspects of his life can find expression in the course of his work. These are aspects of his life which he needs to master if he is to do that work well. But he will not be able to do so unless he can recognize them. My immediate point is that their expression is excluded by his conscious and directed activities — those in which he is concerned to meet certain requirements. This point is a particular instance of Freud's general thesis which I have attempted to illustrate. I suggest that it is this thesis, together with his conception of dreams as the life of the mind during sleep, that justifies Freud in the way he treats dreams in psycho-analysis.

Thus he writes that 'the material of the forgotten childish experiences is accessible to the dream' (1949a, p. 177). In other words, the mind returns to it when, in sleep, it is relatively free from the conscious preoccupations of daily life: 'Our dreams take us back every night to this infantile stage' (p. 178). It is the expressions of this 'infantile mental life' which Freud claims are active to a certain degree in the daily adult life of the individual. Freud holds that dreams mirror this aspect of the mind's life. Its expressions constitute the *meaning* of the dream, although they can only be recognized and so the dream's meaning clarified by the help of 'interpretation'. This, Freud argues, is unlike decoding a message given in an esoteric cypher and involves knowledge of the individual dreamer: 'I am prepared to find that the same piece of content may conceal a different meaning when it occurs in various people or in various contexts' (1966, p. 137). In other words, the interpreter is not guided by any general rule or law. His interpretations come from taking the dream with the dreamer's associations and placing it in the context of his growing knowledge of the dreamer's particular life. Certainly this takes experience — experience acquired through treating other patients (see 1949a, pp. 193—4). But the generality of such experience is not the same as the generality of a rule or law (see Wittgenstein, 1963, p. 227). If I am right, it follows that when Freud denied that 'changes in mental phenomena are guided by *chance*', he was not suggesting that they are governed by laws (see Wittgenstein, 1966, p. 42).

As for Freud's 'essentialism' in connection with dreams, his view that all dreams are wish-fulfilments, this was a relatively early formulation, and it is not easy to know how strictly it is to be taken. Freud, himself, considers this question: 'Why must our thoughts at night be any less many-sided than our thoughts by day? . . . We surely go back on the advance we have made if we try to limit this meaning too strictly' (1949a, p. 187). His answer, as I understand it, comes to this. A dream may give expression to a variety of thoughts and emotions which preoccupy the dreamer in his waking life. But insofar as sleep makes early experiences accessible to the dreamer, it constitutes a 'regressive' experience in the context of which wishing assumes a dominating role. The 'primitive' response to a wish is to imagine it as fulfilled, and the dream is just such a response: 'Insofar as you are considering only the thoughts represented in it, the dream may be any conceivable thing — a warning, a resolve, a preparation, and so on; but besides this, it itself is always the fulfilment of an unconscious wish, and, when you regard it as the result of the dream-work, it is this alone' (1949a, pp. 189—90). This raises further difficulties which are not pertinent to our topic here.

Earlier in this section I compared the vision behind Freud's determinism to the vision of great novelists in whose writings the unity in the actions and reactions of the main characters is presented and studied. I then commented on those acts and passivities which seem 'arbitrary' and on the kind of 'significance' they had for Freud. But what about those masses of ordinary actions which a man performs every day of his life? Does determinism reach here farther than we suppose? What sort of relation do these actions bear to the agent's character and to his *personal* life? Freud did not consider these questions directly, but they are relevant to his determinism. I am thinking of such actions which are certainly 'purposive' but which do not bear any particular intimate relation to his life and character — opening the door to walk out of a room, driving a car to go to work, picking up a pen to write a letter, signing a cheque to draw money from the bank, adding up one's expenses at the end of the week. These are all actions that belong to a way of living, and their sense or identity presupposes much else that equally belongs to that way of living. Rhees once compared the way our neighbour's actions and ours belong to a general way of living with the way our utterances belong to a language. He said: 'You cannot know the relation of a man to his action unless you take into account the way in which the action is understood.' Think, for instance, of a man who forges a signature, or one who refuses to put his signature under a petition or letter of protest. His relation to signing a name, the action which he does or refuses to do, can only be seen and its significance considered if one understands what signing one's name means, how such an action is normally understood by the person in question and others, his neighbours and colleagues. There must be a common measure of understanding though if there is to be any action, if there are to be agents with distinctive personalities, and if our individualities are to come into play and find expression in what we do. This is true not only of a man's strengths and weaknesses, his virtues and vices, but also of his eccentricities. As Rhees said: 'The people we go about among do not all behave reasonably. People are queer. But I find them queer because their actions are actions which mean something. People may say too things which I do not understand. But they say them in a language which I do understand.'

In illustrating what I mean by a man's relation to his actions, a relation in which his individuality finds expression,

I did not pick examples of routine actions done in circumstances about which there is nothing special. I mentioned the man who forges a signature and one who refuses to sign something with which he does not agree. But what about a man who signs a cheque to draw money from the bank, one who opens the door to walk out of the room, or drives a car to work? I think that Freud would have agreed that although such actions are not senseless, there is nevertheless no particular *personal* significance *normally* in a man's performing them. He would say, however, that there is often something significant about a man's way of performing them, something about his style of performance in which his individuality and character find expression — the way he drives his car, the way he parks it, the way he walks into a room, the way he knocks at the door. He would say, as we have already seen, that the more unguarded he is the more will his personality find expression in the way he does these things, although if he is normally guarded, the form this takes in his way of doing them will also speak about the stresses and strains in his personality.

Even here, though, in the domain of styles of performance and styles of expression, linguistic, facial and other, we have to distinguish between what comes from the individual and bears his stamp and what does not. But, once more, if we are to appreciate how much a person's individuality finds expression in his style of performance, in the gestures and phrases which he returns to repeatedly, we must recognize the significance which these have independently of the person in the community in which he lives, the class or group to which he is related. This was Professor Hoggart's question in the first two of his Reith Lectures:

All these are not readings of personality unless you do a second and third translation. Given that this is the pattern of available signals, and that their social meanings are thus and thus, what does that tell us about any particular man . . . at bottom? The justification for learning more about social vocabularies is that unless you understand what social signals you are responding to all the time, you will be less likely to see through to the different personalities, to break up the groups of men of certain ages and styles, and see the individuals within. (1971, p. 676)

This is, surely, one aspect of what Freud was interested in when he spoke of 'the meaningfulness of mental phenomena'. And it would have been of interest to him particularly in the context of psycho-analytic therapy, that is where the analyst listens to the patient with a view to understanding his personal problems, problems which are in part determined by his character, by the stresses and strains in his personality, and, in turn, helping him to recognize and understand them himself.

4   Summary

The question of determinism was confused in Freud's mind with the reign of causality. This further led him to think that it implies that free will is an illusion.

My main concern in this chapter has been to show that Freud's determinism has in reality little to do with causality or with the reign of law in the sphere of the mind. The order which Freud glimpsed there is of a different nature. I have tried to elucidate what it amounts to. Certainly it does not add up to anything uniform.

As for his idea that free will is an illusion, even though this may come from confusion, is there not something important in it? This is the question I turn to in the next chapter.

10

Determinism and the Freedom of the Will

1 The Scope and Limits of Human Bondage

Freud's denial of the freedom of the will has a life independent of the confusions I pointed out in the last chapter. It also comes from his recognition of the extent to which men are ruled by forces within them, constituted by their own nature and character, which they neither recognize nor can control: 'The ego is not master in its own house' (1950, vol. iv, p. 355). This denial can be seen as an attempt to draw attention to continuities that we generally overlook in the hope of altering our apprehension of men and their plight. The words 'We are never free' are sometimes so used as to express some insight into life, representing human actions and relations in the light of certain ideals or paradigms. In 'Freewill' Wisdom gives two such examples. In the first these words are meant to initiate a new way of considering physical motion:

> Imagine a time when scientific knowledge is very rudimentary. A man is washing a carriage. He jacks up one wheel and sets it spinning. Although he has often done this before he is now struck by the fact that the wheel though it isn't touching the ground and isn't hindered by mud or water or brakes slows down and stops. He asks himself 'Why does it stop when there is nothing to stop it?' and then he answers his own question by saying 'There is something to stop it — air. And air is like water.' But now if this philosophical scientist goes about saying 'No wheel on earth ever really turns freely' he is likely to be misunderstood.

Other people who still use the words 'moving freely' in the way they always have been used, that is, to distinguish between a wheel or a pendulum which is moving unhindered by anything but air and one which is moving in water or milk or oil, may misunderstand him. Some of them may think that he means that whenever people have distinguished between one thing and another by saying 'This is moving freely, that is not' they have been mistaken. Others may say, 'No. He cannot be saying anything which is so plainly false. He has without warning changed the use of words, and when he says "Nothing really moves freely" all he means is that every movement has some explanation.' Both these interpretations are wrong. The philosophical scientist whom we have imagined is neither denying the important differences which have so far been marked by saying 'This is moving freely, that is not', nor asserting merely that for every movement there is some explanation. He is beginning to point out the affinities between, for example, a wheel turning in the air and a wheel turning in water or milk or oil. (1965, pp. 28–9)

One could say that he wishes to offer a new method of representation, a new way of plotting and describing the motion of objects in terms of the forces acting on them. Remember Galileo and Newton. In their case 'a body moving freely' was an ideal that could be realized only in thought; it was a norm used in describing how bodies actually move – where the deviation from the norm is what is important for the calculations that are carried out. In this sense the words 'Nothing really moves freely' express a statement of grammar and so do not convey anything about what is the case in contrast with what might have been. On the other hand, they open up new possibilities. For although they set out a new geometry of motion, the *use* of that geometry will enable us to say and see new things, give us a new conception of how bodies actually move in contrast with how they might have done.

Wisdom next goes on to point out that similarly someone who says, 'No one ever really acts freely' may not wish to deny important differences which we mark when we say such things as 'He was quite free in the matter, she was not', but may be 'taking a first step towards drawing our attention to certain affinities between some or all of those actions we

have so far called "free" and those we have called "not free" '
(1965, p. 29). He then asks: What are the affinities which
such a man may be trying to draw attention to? He may wish
to draw attention to affinities between cases where a man
obeys the orders of someone who has hypnotized him, cases
where a man imposes his will on another, and cases where the
voice which a man speaks and the will with which he acts are
not his own:

> Sometimes a man dies without ever having been more than
> half himself without having become free. In Marquand's novel,
> *H. M. Pulham Esq.*, a young man finds in a New York adver-
> tising firm a very different life from what he was used to at
> home and at his school. At the office he meets a man and a
> woman and he likes them both although the outlook of each
> of them is very different from his own and that of this family.
> The woman he comes to want to marry. She feels a difference
> between them and hesitates. Then his father dies, he returns
> to his home town and takes up his father's business and marries
> a girl his family would regard as thoroughly suitable. All goes
> well, they have two children, they are fond of each other, they
> are, he insists, happy together. But the story is a subtle study of
> how far in his life he is himself and how far he never is. (1965,
> pp. 31–2)

We ought to contrast the case where such a young man
returns to his home town and we say, 'He has found himself'
and the case where he does so and we say 'He has never been
able to break out, to free himself from the restricting influence of his parents, that stifling atmosphere which he carries
with him wherever he goes.' The contrast is important, even
though there are mixed cases in an intermediate position
between those contrasted. But the man who says, 'No one is
really free' need not deny this contrast; and even if he does,
what he says may still be worth while for noting affinities
between post-hypnotic action and men and women who have
not outgrown their dependence on their parents and who are
ruled by voices from their childhood.

When Freud said that 'our mental life is subject to determinism' he was *in part* speaking in this way. The fact that he
was *also* saying that everything we do has an explanation

should not lead us to ignore this. So we could say that Freud's determinism combines two different sets of claims which need to be distinguished from each other. One of these centres around his vision of the 'meaningfulness of even the apparently most obscure and arbitrary mental phenomena', while at the heart of the other is his vision of the scope of 'unconscious determination' in human life.

2 'Inner Freedom' and Outer Circumstances

This second aspect of Freud's determinism involves certain confusions even if treated as an eye-opener in the way I suggested. Therefore, if we are to learn from it, to appreciate the affinities and continuities it brings to our attention, those we do not make enough of in our considerations of people, we must not lose sight of the contrasts from which the terms in which he speaks derive their meaning.

The idea of a 'free man' may call to mind many different things. One may think of a man who is not in gaol, one who is not chained, one who is not a slave. 'At last I am free.' A man may say this when his door has been unlocked, his chains undone. He may say it when a marriage that has become a burden to him is dissolved. He may say it on landing in a country that has given him political asylum. In this sense a man is free who is not chained, oppressed, hounded, gagged.

The man who is chained, threatened, blackmailed, dictated to: is he unfree because he is unable to do what he would have done otherwise, or because he yields to pressure, cannot remain independent and stand his ground? Both considerations enter into the way we speak here. The latter recognizes that even when a man is in chains he can remain free in spirit and call his soul his own. A slave, for instance, who has no option but to do what he is told need not act in servility. And both Kierkegaard and Simone Weil have pointed out that there is such a thing as the voluntary acceptance of involuntary suffering. In his ability to bear such suffering patiently a man can remain independent of it, avoid being reduced to the status of a thing. Freedom here characterizes the spirit in which he suffers. This spirit which Kierkegaard describes as 'patience' has to be distinguished from 'passivity'.

Certainly external conditions can restrict a man's freedom of action, and in the extreme case they can reduce it practically to nil. But even then he can remain free in the attitude he takes towards these conditions. He can yield to them and go under or he can take a stand towards them, even if this consists in a resolve to accept them. For in the latter case the resolve comes from him, the attitude is his; it is not something imposed on him by the circumstances. Where external conditions leave him some latitude of action, we speak of him as having acted freely where he acts in a spirit of independence. Thus in the face of danger, threats, coercion or intimidation he does what *he* wants to do, what he thinks right; he remains true to his promises or ideals, and, therefore, to himself. On the other hand, to avert some danger a man may do something which he would otherwise not have chosen to do. He may part with his wallet when threatened at the point of a gun and still do so of his own free will. This is what under the particular adverse circumstances he chooses to do; it is what in those circumstances he thinks it right to do. In acting this way he doesn't go against his own better judgment, he doesn't compromise any deeply held conviction. If he had acted in a cowardly way, if he had been mastered by the desire to save his life and prepared to give in to it whatever the cost, that would be different.[1]

The man who hands his wallet to the highwayman is acting under duress. He might express this by saying: 'I did not give it away freely.' But we could still say that despite the threat his 'inner freedom' remained intact. We mean that he did not allow his fear to cloud his judgment and that he did not act against his will. Thus if the situation were a different one and the gunman was an enemy soldier asking him to reveal a military secret he would not have done so. In neither case does he relinquish his freedom, become an instrument to an alien will. To keep it one has to fight, to resist pressure and even be prepared to give up one's life. Hence the idea of

---

[1] We should not forget that sometimes obstinacy, resistance, the refusal to give in are 'reaction-formations' and, as such, not expressions of a free spirit.

freedom as something valued, something that calls for strength, integrity, resourcefulness and independence of spirit. Hence Nietzsche says that freedom is measured 'by the resistance which has to be overcome, by the effort it costs to stay *aloft*' (1972, p. 92). Certainly the man who pampers himself, who is used to taking the easy way out, will fail to measure up to such a test.

Sartre goes so far as to say that where no demands are made on his loyalty, courage and integrity, a man will tend to sink into a humdrum existence in which he is not fully himself, and acts in slavery to habit:

> We were never more free than during the German occupation. We had lost our rights, beginning with the right to talk. Everyday we were insulted to our faces and had to take it in silence . . . Everywhere, on bill boards, in newspapers, on the screen, we encountered the revolting and insipid picture of ourselves that our oppressors wanted us to accept. And, because of this, we were free. Because the Nazi venom seeped even into our thoughts, every accurate thought was a conquest. Because an all-powerful police tried to force us to hold our tongues, every word took on the value of a declaration of principles. Because we were hunted down, every one of our gestures had the weight of a solemn commitment. The circumstances, atrocious as they often were, finally made it possible for us to live, without pretence or false shame, the hectic and impossible existence that is known as the lot of man. (1949, pp. 11–12)

When Sartre speaks of 'the hectic and impossible existence that is known as the lot of man' there is a value judgment implicit in what he says. His claim is that unless we can measure up to that 'hectic and impossible existence' we shall not live with dignity — the dignity without which each of us is less of a man. In other words, Sartre refuses to call a man a man unless he lives with dignity and remains an individual — and these are value judgments. Therefore he regards the circumstances in which this dignity flourishes as necessary to a man's existence as a man.

Compare with Frankl's comment when writing about his experiences in a concentration camp: 'Every day, every hour, offered the opportunity to make a decision, a decision which determined whether you would or would not submit to those powers which threatened to rob you of your very self, your inner freedom; which determined whether or not you would become the plaything of circumstances, renouncing freedom and dignity to become moulded into the form of the typical inmate' (1967, p. 104). The typical inmate, in this sense, is an antithesis of what Sartre calls 'a man'. Frankl goes on to say that he became acquainted with some exceptional people 'whose behaviour in camp, whose suffering and death, bore witness to the fact that the last inner freedom cannot be lost' (p. 105). His point is that it is not the extreme conditions in the camp that make the majority of the inmates into 'the typical inmate', but what attitude they take towards these conditions. That is up to each man. However, while this is indeed up to each man, is such a choice really always open to each man? In other words, even if one were to agree that a man's 'outer conditions' cannot make him relinquish his 'inner freedom', one may wonder whether a man is always free to surmount those conditions, whether it is always in his power to do so.

Sartre's answer here is as uncompromising as the determinist's. While I think that it contains an important corrective to the determinist's view, it is nevertheless not the only alternative to determinism. In other words, from the view that man has it in him to surmount the most extreme of conditions, if only by accepting them, it does not follow that every man can in fact surmount them. To put it more generally, from the conceptual claim that man has free will it does not follow that every man can in fact exercise his will freely in the choices that face him — any more than it follows from the claim that 'man is a rational animal' that men always act rationally.

3 Antitheses of Human Freedom

Freud, I suggested, is wrong to deny that man has free will. But he had much light to shed on the particular cases where men fail to exercise their will freely. He increased our understanding of their variety and opened our eyes to their scope. Let us try to take a synoptic view of them and ask ourselves: What does this failure amount to in each case? In what sense does it constitute a curtailment of human freedom?

There are, to begin with, different forms of compulsion and constraint that operate on the will. Generally we can say that if the will is constrained a man will be unable to do what he wants, has the knowledge and ability to do. Where it is compelled, he acts against his will. What constitutes the constraint or compulsion has to be something 'external' to the will. But what does 'external' mean where the constraint is an overmastering fear, the compulsion an overpowering need? Besides what are the words 'overmastering' and 'overpowering' meant to signify? The magnitude of the fear, the strength of the need, or the weakness of the will? Let us look at particular cases.

Take the case where men are described as acting in slavery to habit and subservience to authority. Here we have in mind the mindlessness with which such men act so that they cannot be described as doing what they want. The point is that doing what one wants takes thought. Having a mind of one's own, then, seems to be a precondition of freedom of action. This is not simply a matter of enlightenment, however, but of independence of personality or spirit. Thus subservience to authority is generally a form of dependence and often involves the fear of contradicting it.

Where a man's slavery to fear has become habitual we speak of cowardice. What the coward lacks is not a mind of his own, but courage. This involves an inner strength which stems from belief in oneself. But such a belief needs to be distinguished from arrogance. It is not a belief in the 'ego'.

Where slavery to need and desire has become habitual we often speak of incontinence. In doing so we suggest that the fault lies with the person, without necessarily blaming him for it. We say that he is weak in his will, meaning that he is easily dislodged from his resolve. Sometimes, however, we describe the need or desire as 'irresistible' implying that many others would not be able to resist it if they were subject to it. But such comparisons are notoriously difficult to make. Various addictions would exemplify the kind of slavery in question; but the history of their formation and development would be relevant.

Particular situations in which a man is overcome by fear and acts in panic, loses his temper and says or does something which he regrets, or is mastered by jealousy and 'loses his reason', throw some light on the 'logic' of the above kind of case. These are instances of slavery not so much to continuous needs as to passions of the moment — even when, as in the case of jealousy, the passion is not short-lived. The man in question may say that he lost his head, meaning that his judgment was clouded by his emotions.

Connected is the case where a man gives in to a temptation. He loses sight of considerations that normally weigh with him; he is mastered by a desire of the moment. I shall say more about the lack of control in these cases later.

Impulsive actions in which a person is moved by what belongs to the moment are obviously related to those where a man is ruled by a passion evoked in him by a particular situation. He gives in to an impulse, and so while the action satisfies the impulse it does not come from him: it is not responsible to anything that he cares for deeply, and it ignores a consideration of possible effects and consequences. Freud would say that the action is determined by the unconscious. In other words, what the moment touches in him, the purpose and considerations it mobilizes, are not part of the kind of unity from which he acts when he acts responsibly. 'It is determined by the moment', 'It is determined by the unconscious', 'It does not come from him' — these descriptions belong together. Freud certainly recognizes that impulsiveness is antithetical to self-mastery and that without the latter a person is like a ship without a captain, at the mercy of the waves without or the whims of a crew within who have fallen out with each other, not guided by a knowledge of navigation or a concern for the safety of the passengers.

In some ways the man who in everything prefers to take the easy way out and who deliberately pursues a life of pleasure is like the impulsive person. His hedonism is the nearest thing he can concoct to give substance to an empty life, one devoid of any genuine concern. He may think that he does just what he likes and that he is free for not being shackled by attachments and dependencies. But this is an illusion betrayed by his reluctance to take a stand on anything that would involve him in strife, conflict and unpleasantness. His position, unlike Plato's Callicles who was not an hedonist, comes from weakness, not from strength. My reasons for claiming that he lacks freedom are twofold: he has very little for the sake of which to act and his actions are a form of yielding.

The man subject to obsessions, insofar as he is ruled by a fixed idea, is unfree. He has to trim his actions, devote his energies to something that does not make sense in terms of the things he believes in and cares for. Like a slave who is at the beck and call of a master who is not concerned about him. Akin to the case of compulsions and addictions is the case of men who are a slave to their ambitions, to greed, cruelty or masochism. These differ from ordinary compulsions in that the man subject to them does what he wants. In Freudian jargon, they are 'ego syntonic', they are expressions of the man's character. But in that case why should they be regarded as a form of compulsion? In what sense can the man subject to them be said to act in slavery?[2]

Akin to these are those cases where a man cannot avoid taking a placatory attitude towards others, cannot tell them what he thinks and where they get off. He is submissive, gives in to them, and feels he has to, though he resents it. He feels he can kick himself for it. Here, clearly, in acting in character he is acting against his will. Similarly we have the case of the man who is unable to go along with anyone else's suggestion or obey an authority. He takes even the fulfilment of a contractual obligation as a threat to the independence of his will. He is a perpetual rebel, unable to co-operate with anyone unless he feels he has the initiative. In both cases we are dealing with 'reaction-formations' where the agent has to subordinate his actions to a posture of denial, especially in situations that threaten to force what he cannot tolerate in himself to his attention. The submissive man yields his

---

[2] For a discussion of these questions see Dilman 1983, chapter 7, 'Development and Character'.

autonomy to others, and he does so begrudgingly, driven to do so by anxieties rooted in phantasies of omnipotence. Understandably he suffers from a feeling of impotence. The rebel, on the other hand, does not yield anything to other people's demands and feels in charge of every situation. But he is not, insofar as his rebelliousness is as much something dictated to him by his unconscious needs as the former man's submissiveness. He does not refuse to comply with a demand because of its content, but because it is a demand – or so he imagines.

In some ways similar is the case of the man who nurses a grudge, or one with a chip on his shoulder. He is a captive of the past, of something that happened and is over with, though he cannot forget it. He subordinates everything to the demand it makes on him. We must be careful to distinguish this kind of case from the case of a man whose concern for what he has done in the past imposes a limitation on his present life which he willingly embraces. It may be something he has done for which he feels deep remorse, or something that has happened to him, such as the loss of a loved one, for whom he still grieves. Freud distinguished between such cases only superficially. Thus of grief and mourning he said: 'We rest assured that after a lapse of time it will be overcome' (1950, vol. iv, p. 153). Almost as if what distinguishes mourning from melancholia is that the former is a temporary condition. Whereas with grief and remorse something new enters into a man's life. They are both expressions of acceptance – the acceptance of something that cannot be changed. Yet, paradoxically, that acceptance is a form of liberation. (I have discussed this question in Dilman, 1976.) In contrast, nursing a grudge and vindictiveness are ways of clinging to one's past personality. Here it may be the person's unwillingness or inability to forgive that holds him captive.

A very different kind of case is that of the man who rushes into schemes which easily rouse his enthusiasm without much awareness of the difficulties in the way of realizing them. Such a man is not pushed into anything against his will; nor is there anything external to his will preventing him from realizing what attracts him. Nor is he like the man who does what he himself regrets because he cannot control his impulses. Rather his perserverance does not match his enthusiasm. For this reason we would describe that enthusiasm as shallow. It is an enthusiasm that does not want to know and deal with difficulties. He is so impatient to get to what attracts him that he cannot avail himself of the means necessary to get there. What attracts him engages only his fancy — and that is unamenable to discipline. To use a simile, he is like a car which cannot make progress because its tyres have no tread on them to hold the road. Such a man is not free to make progress in the direction to which he points; he lacks self-mastery. Yet he does not act in slavery to anything. What holds him back is the lack of grit. Here we cannot speak of compulsion or constraint.

Then again we have the man whose life is not his own and whose actions do not come from him — they are not determined by him. He may have no thoughts of his own and is easily led by others. He acts in subjection to public opinion. His tastes are determined by the trend setters, the popular press, the advertisers. Yet we cannot say that he is compelled to go after the things he pursues; he does not act against his will — unlike the man who acts in subservience to authority. We cannot say that he is prevented from doing what he wants. His trouble is that he doesn't know what he wants, he has no mind of his own. He is not even able to pose the question of what he wants for himself. Being under the illusion of living his own life he cannot search for self-knowledge. We cannot speak of him as free, not because of any constraints on his will or any compulsion on it, but because his will is not his own. I mentioned earlier Huxley's allegory of a 'Brave New World'. This was meant to warn us against what we are on the road to becoming: we may be manipulated 'from inside' by a society we have developed ourselves — 'the great beast'. This is a powerful picture of slavery; yet no ordinary picture of it.

There is too the case of the man who is divided in his will. Whatever he does he cannot do what he wants to do. Such a man has to find out what he wants to do before he can be free. Yet this is not finding something that is hidden from him, waiting to be discovered. Finding out what he wants

involves the resolution of an inner division and is, in some
ways, like making up one's mind. It differs from an ordinary
decision, however, in that it involves what Professor Taylor
calls a 'radical evaluation', in other words an evaluation or
revaluation of one's values, and in that sense an examination
of one's most fundamental attitudes. (See Taylor, 1977, and
the discussion of this in chapter 7, section 3 above.) But in
most such cases much has to be discarded by way of illusions,
prejudices and defensive postures before these attitudes
become accessible for examination.

What does this review of the antitheses to human freedom
show us? It shows us, first, that we cannot understand what
lack of freedom means in every case in the same terms, for
instance in terms of the constraint or· compulsion of the
human will — a man unable to carry out what it is his will to
do or compelled to act against his will. Even in cases which
we can understand in these terms, there is the question of
how a will that is his is determined: what does 'self-determination' mean? Thus one form which the lack of freedom
takes is the failure, on the part of a man who knows his
mind, to translate his will into action, to execute his intentions. He may fail to do so through fear. But what does it
take to execute one's intentions, to remain unfaithful to
one's commitments, in the face of obstacles? Not always
the same thing — as we see in different cases of such failures.
Sometimes we speak of a man lacking self-control, as when
he cannot control his temper. Sometimes we say that he
lacks courage. Sometimes we say that he lacks perserverance.

The cases where we may describe him as lacking resolve
shade into those cases where we may describe him as not
knowing his mind. This opens up a vista on a variety of cases
where we can no longer presuppose a will which we can
describe as constrained or compelled. Thus I spoke of the
man who has no mind of his own, the man whose will is
manipulated 'from inside', the man who is divided in his
will, the man who lacks whatever it takes to back up his
expressions of enthusiasm. Very roughly, while in the former
cases he is the captain of his ship, his hands are tied, or
he has lost control of his ship; in the latter cases he is not

even the captain of his ship, though he cherishes the illusion that he is.

4   Freedom and its Dimensions

We reminded ourselves of the variety of connections in which we deny that a man is free and noted some of the ways in which he may himself be mixed up in the conditions that constitute his lack of freedom. Appreciating this variety is important in an evaluation of the kind of determinism with which we are concerned.

The occasions on which we ask whether a man is free are varied and on each occasion we have special reasons for raising the question. The claim that a man is free relates to these questions which vary from case to case. Without the special surroundings in which such questions are raised the claim that a man is free, just like that, makes no sense.

Professor Austin went as far as to suggest that the positive assertion is in reality a denial: '"Free" is only used to rule out the suggestion of some or all of its recognised antitheses' (Austin, 1961, p. 128). 'The negative word marks the abnormality, while the positive word serves to rule out the suggestion of that abnormality' (p. 140). Thus in a particular case 'I am free' may be equivalent to 'I am not engaged'. In another case 'He left of his own free will' may mean 'He was not thrown out'. In yet another case 'He gave the money freely' may mean 'He had no ulterior motives'. While this is true and important, it does not take us far enough in our search for the connections on which the determinist builds his case.

Austin points out that a man is free, for instance, if he is not acting under duress. All right. But why do we describe him as 'unfree' when he acts under duress? Perhaps because he acts differently from the way he would have acted otherwise. And that may be just the way he would have liked to act, or the way he wants to act. Here then 'He is free' may mean 'He is doing what he wants' — a positive assertion. For Austin, questions about freedom focus our attention on what checks or restraints a man in his actions. But something is a restraint only relative to what opposes it; a compulsion is a compulsion relative to what resists it — relative to the course of action from which it deflects a man. This is presupposed when a man is described as acting in slavery to a compulsion, or where we say that his character has become a strait-jacket. Hence beside Austin's question, 'What is being denied when a man is said to be free?', we have to put the complementary question, 'What is being denied when he is said not to be free?' There doesn't seem to be much room in Austin's account for the notion of freedom as an *achievement* and of its lack as a *failure*.

On Austin's view the occasions on which men are unfree must be the exception rather than the rule — they are so in our use of language. It is only in special circumstances that a man is said not to be free: 'The negative word marks the abnormality.' Again Austin's point is an important one. The circumstances in which he originally learnt to perform various actions and to choose between different courses of action are the *normal* circumstances where in doing these actions a man acts freely. I do not think, however, that this invalidates the kind of determinism under consideration. For although each case in which we are justified in describing a man as unfree is *conceptually* an exceptional case, in the sense that we understand it as a deviation from a conceptual norm to which it constitutes an antithesis, it does not follow that such cases may not *in fact* constitute the rule rather than the exception. I suggested that this is all that Freud claims to be the case.

It is true that of the various occasions on which a man may be said to be unfree those on which he does or decides something are of special interest to us. But it is important to note that a man may also be said to be unfree in the way he lives, thinks and behaves, in his affective responses, and in the way he expresses himself. Thus his fear of displeasing someone may prevent a man from expressing his thoughts freely. Such a man will fail to be frank. If his responses are subservient to his desire to please, we might say that they are not spontaneous, that he lacks spontaneity. If in his actions he is too concerned to avoid consequences that evoke anxiety in him, we may say that they express more what he fears than what he wants. This does not mean that free action is not subject to thought and considerations. As we have already seen, impulsive action which is not subject to thought is one of the antitheses of free action. Both thought and feeling have a role to play in action, and neither in itself can be said to curtail a man's freedom in action. On the contrary, the absence of thought makes a man impulsive, and the absence of feeling makes him stilted. The difficulty lies in understanding how they are combined in free actions, those that come from the self and accord with a man's free will. Again a man who, in one kind of case, is said not to have been able to consider some matter freely may be one who is prejudiced. If he is free in his thinking then he has an open mind – he is unbiased, he doesn't have an axe to grind.

Freedom, then, has many dimensions, and the criteria of what counts as freedom vary from one case to another. The form which freedom takes depends on the dimension in question. Thus, as we have seen, frankness, spontaneity, courage, autonomy, an open mind, are some expressions of freedom in its different dimensions. It should not be taken for granted that what curtails a man's freedom in one dimension necessarily curtails it in another. A man, for instance, whose emotional development has been stunted will not have the same choices open to him as he would have had if he had developed freely. But within the choices that are open to him in a particular situation, can he not make a free decision? The answer to this question is not clear cut and I shall return to it further on. Again, a person may be free to do a different action from the one he decides to do, he may alter his decisions, revise his plans. But, for all this, he may fail to act differently. He may pursue a course of action diametrically opposed to one he has pursued earlier and regretted. Yet he may do so in the same spirit as before, fail to avoid earlier mistakes. The case of Father Sergius in Tolstoy's story is a case in point. He leaves the service of the Czar and enters a monastery in the hope of leading a different kind of life. But for a very long time the vanity and ambitiousness of his earlier life plague his life in the monastery. As Schopenhauer puts it: 'On looking back over our past, we see at once that our life consists of mere variations on one and the same theme, namely, our character, and that the same fundamental bass sounds through it all' (1951, part vi, p. 63). But here 'He cannot act differently' does not mean that he couldn't have done something different from what he in fact did in the sense which, as we have seen, concerned Moore.

Moore was concerned with 'freedom of action' whereas Schopenhauer's interest lies in man's freedom to make something of himself — to make of himself what he wills, given the ideals to which he has given his heart. If I understand him rightly, Schopenhauer does not think that character cannot change. What he thinks is that a man cannot act differently from the way he does until he becomes other than he is (1951, part vi, p. 56). This is not a truism, as it may seem to be. Every character offers some resistance to change; but until there is a desire to change, there will be nothing it can be said to resist. As we shall see later, a person's character can be described as restricting his freedom only when it is predominantly defensive, or when it is a form of defence.[3] Generally, it is 'immature' forms of character that sound 'the same fundamental bass' through men's lives which Proust described as *'le plagiat de soi-même'* (the plagiarism of oneself). My immediate point at the moment, however, is that here we have a different dimension of freedom, a different dimension along which men's freedom is often curtailed, from the one to which Moore's and Austin's problems relate.

5   *Moral Necessity and Weakness of the Will*

We saw earlier that both Freud and Ernest Jones claimed that our conviction that we have free will 'does not manifest itself in weighty and important decisions'. With such decisions 'one has much more the feeling of a psychic compulsion and gladly falls back upon it' (Freud, 1954b, p. 212), one feels 'irresistibly impelled', one feels that one 'really has no choice in the matter, nor desires to have any' (Jones, 1974, p. 182).

---

[3] For a discussion of this see Dilman 1983, chapter 7, section 2.

Both of them cite Luther's words to the Diet of Worms as an example: 'Here I stand, I cannot do anything else.' Ernest Jones adds: 'And if one asked a man why he chose to risk his life at some critical juncture he would mostly reply: "I couldn't help it. I just had to".' Both writers confuse this with e.g. the kleptomaniac's avowal: 'I couldn't help taking it. I saw it there and felt I just had to take it.'

In fact, however, they are diametrically opposed. The kleptomaniac's words are an expression of impotence; they are the words of someone who has yielded to an overpowering impulse. Luther's words, on the other hand, are an expression of conviction. When his actions come from this conviction he is at one with himself. The conviction defines his identity. That is the meaning of his words, 'Here I stand': 'Take that away from me and I am nothing', 'I cannot depart from it and continue to be the man I am', 'I have no choice; I can do no other'. These words do not imply that one is not acting on one's own behalf, that one is acting under duress, that if one were left to oneself one would act differently. The action in question is neither involuntary, nor against one's will. In fact, very much the contrary is the case. Why then does one use words which suggest otherwise?

Given the moral character of what one is asked to do, one has no choice. Once that is clear, there is no further question for one about how one may nevertheless benefit in going along with it or what one may lose in refusing. For the man who has given his heart to certain moral values, the moral character of what is in question is a 'compelling consideration'. This refers to the 'absolute' character of moral considerations, to the 'indivisibility' of the good. In other words, nothing can compensate for the fact that the proposed action involves some evil. Thus for the man who genuinely values truth and honesty, an action which he judges to be dishonest would be *ruled out*. This is what his words, 'I have no choice' signify.

Its being ruled out for him and his not wanting to do it coincide completely. Here 'I cannot' and 'I will not' express the same thought. 'Why won't you do it?' 'Because I don't want to' trivializes the matter. It is not a question of whether *I* want to or not. The appeal is not to what one wants, but to the moral character of what is at stake. It is *that* which compels one to act, *that* which is contrasted with what the agent wants. It does not compel him to act against his will; it determines his will in the sense of providing him with compelling considerations. What the situation demands from him, given his moral beliefs, and what he wants to do are one and the same. The words, 'I have to', emphasize that it is not a matter of just what he happens to want, not a whim or arbitrary matter.

The choice of the words we are trying to understand is related to the way in which an agent's moral values determine his purposes, the way they are related to what he wants. Where in the cases that interest us a man says, 'This is what I *must* do' or 'I *cannot* do such-and-such', he is emphasizing that his reasons are not relative to what he wants. It is rather the other way around, what he wants to do in the particular circumstances is determined by the reasons that weigh with him. These are provided by the aspect under which he sees those circumstances. He sees them under that aspect because he thinks of them in terms of certain moral concepts. What he sees moves him to action, or rules out certain actions for him, because of the values that matter to him. Those values are neither an end to which he aims, nor a means to the realization of something that he wants independently of them. They provide him with a norm in terms of which he evaluates the situation in which he acts and the actions he considers in those situations. He sees the course of action on which he decides in a particular situation as a requirement of particular values that matter to him. Hence his words: 'I must.' What he does is not what *he* wants, but what those *values* demand.

These values are implicit in his thoughts, but their realization is not something that he aims at. Thus Simone Weil says that moral action is pure when one acts out of compulsion or moral necessity, rather than attraction. The genuinely compassionate man, for instance, is not moved by the thought of doing good, but simply by the pity he feels for the person in need of help: 'I *cannot* walk away and leave him in the lurch.' In contrast, someone who says, 'I have decided to help him', thereby suggests that he has weighed the alternatives and on balance has chosen this particular one. For the compassionate man, on the other hand, once the plight of the person in need of help is clear, there is no alternative.

The way he is compelled by his compassion is diametrically opposed to the way someone may be compelled by his rage to strike a man, or by something that attracts him irresistably. In the former case the compassion he feels determines his will; he is at one with it. Thus if he ignores it, he will blame himself, he will feel remorse. If it can be said to 'prevent' him from doing anything, this will be an action in which he yields to a desire which he himself condemns. It is, therefore, in acting in accordance with such a desire that he acts unfreely. Whereas in resisting it he is able to remain true to everything that he stands by. Thus though he may be described as being compelled by his compassion, this does not mean that he acts unfreely. On the contrary, his action constitutes one of the paradigms of a free action. Let us imagine that going to the other man's rescue involves a danger that frightens him. In overcoming or ignoring this fear he acts whole-heartedly. He acts in spite of his fear, but not against his will. Being the man he is, caring for the things he cares for, he can only be behind the course of action dictated by the compassion he feels. If his fear were to get the better of him, he would no longer see his way clearly, or what he might still see he would see as in a dream; it would have lost its grip on his will.

In the previous section I mentioned the expression, 'I lost my head'. A man may use this expression retrospectively when he is overcome by fear, rage, or the appeal of something that greatly attracts him. But not when he is compelled by the compassion he feels, not even when the actions that issue from it lead to the loss of something for which he has worked hard. He considers that to be the price for his beliefs. His attitude to it is very different from his attitude towards the consequences of giving in to his fear or rage. The latter are akin to impulses that are external to his will; whereas the compassion he feels is internally related to it. That is why it cannot be represented as a compulsion on the will. This is not what the words 'compelled by the compassion he feels' mean. In any case, a man who is 'compelled' or 'ruled' by compassion does not act blindly or irresponsibly. He has to be realistic about the other person's needs and practical with regard to the means of helping him. He has to use judgment and discrimination in translating the compassion he feels into action. Otherwise this compassion is little more than an impulse or an exuberance of the self.

When a person, in a particular situation, fails to act in accordance with his values, where what he should do is clear to him, we say that he has yielded to a temptation. Perhaps he puts his self-interest first, or something that attracts him turns him away from what he belives he ought to do. This need not mean that his profession is not sincere, that his beliefs are not genuine. But if they are, then his action is a *lapse*. For in doing it he betrays what he, himself, stands for. The action may be intentional, but it cannot be said to come from him. He *cannot* follow it through, endorse its consequences, and continue to be the person he is. Therefore if he endorses the action, without deceiving himself about its character, this must be short-lived. It is in this sense that though intentional, the action is a lapse. It is not what *he* would do, being the man he is and believing in the things he believes.

How then does he manage to do and endorse it at the moment of engagement? He does so because he is dazzled by what attracts him at the time, or because he is numbed by the fear or anxiety of what would happen to him if he stuck to his beliefs. He acts as in a swoon; what comes over him prevents him from being himself. We could say that at the time of the action he stopped being himself. In yielding to the temptation he does not act as himself — himself as defined by the things he cares for and believes in. We attribute this to an eclipse of his moral consciousness or active self.

It is different where the tempation is not accidental but represents some desire or inclination to which he is prone and to which he continually surrenders. I speak of 'temptation' advisedly, for he does not endorse the actions that stem from it — not for long, not in any sustained sense. Otherwise we would say that his moral professions were insincere, or expressions of self-deception. If we agreed with such a person's judgments and professions, we could say: 'He sees what he has to do and realizes what it means not to do so, yet he is unable to carry it through.' This is one clear-cut case of 'weakness of the will'.

Here the person is unfree, acts in slavery to a desire or fear, not so much because he is compelled, as because he is unable to stand up to or resist temptation. It is the self that lacks, perhaps has never achieved, sufficient inner unity, coherence, or effective organization. The person does have genuine moral beliefs; but what he can put into them is only fragmentary. Consequently the sustenance he derives from them is not enough to hold him together. So when he is subject to temptation or fear there is not enough of himself with which to resist the temptation or stand up against the fear. As he goes under he further loses the self-respect necessary to face up to these problems.

In the earlier cases we saw that if a person was to achieve greater freedom in his life and actions he had to achieve greater self-mastery. Here what is lacking is something more fundamental, although it is not sharply separated from the lack of self-mastery. I have called it lack of self-unity or coherence of the self, and, obviously, what it amounts to needs further discussion. But weakness of the will is an expression of this. Here the will is not simply divided; there is not enough of the person behind it. So it is unable to carry him along at times of difficulty.

6 Summary

I have tried to point out how manifold are the conditions that shackle human life in its different dimensions. This is what Freud's determinism highlights. In appreciating its message it is important not to lose sight of the freedom possible for and actually enjoyed by human beings. Unless we understand this, what sense can we make of the claim that it doesn't exist?

The fact that human freedom, in its many aspects, admits of degree, and so is continuously related to its antitheses, is one of the chief contributors to the idea that it does not exist, and even that we cannot think of it without contradiction. Compare with Socrates' 'No two logs are perfectly equal', which may seem to suggest that no two 'sensible objects' are equal, or can ever be. However, when purged of the confusion it embodies, this claim in the *Phaedo* can be seen to come from reflection on the relation between our descriptions of physical things and mathematics.

I have argued that Freud's determinism, in its bearing on questions relating to human freedom, issues from reflection on the actual conditions of human beings. In the way it sheds light on their plight it resembles those other extravagant claims in philosophy, like Socrates' claim above, which shed light on more purely conceptual matters.

11

Freedom and Autonomy

In the last chapter we saw that Freud did not wish to maintain that men can never act freely, but that they often lack the mastery over their lives which they suppose they have. He thought that if a man cannot be said to think for himself and act on his own behalf, he must be acting in subjection to something external to his will.

We reviewed some of the forms which such subjection takes and noted some of its insidious varieties. We are familiar with the case where a man acts out of fear. Here he may say: 'I did not want to do what I did; I lost my head.' This is different from the case where the fear he feels before some danger does not master him and the consideration of the danger enters into what he does. Again we know of cases where a man acts in subjection to an overpowering desire or emotion provoked by a particular situation. He may himself say: 'I couldn't resist doing what I did, although I knew that I would regret it bitterly as, in fact, I do.' Or he may find, negatively, that where he wishes to speak most he dries up, where he wants to act his will is paralysed, that he cannot do or bring himself to do what he wants to do most. These are cases where he himself feels that his hand is forced or tied, that his action does not issue from his will, or that he has no say about it. Here we can talk of the will being compelled or constrained by something external to it even though the source of the compulsion or constraint is not anything outside the person.

I have discussed elsewhere the sense in which a temptation to which a moral man yields is external to his will even though in yielding to it he satisfies his own desire (see Dilman, 1979, pp. 141—4). Briefly, the desire does not represent his will in the sense that he is not behind it. The connection between him and the desire is purely contingent; his doing what satisfies it is a 'lapse'. We can compare it to a slip of the tongue, however revealing such a slip may be. In contrast, the conviction which fails to restrain him, the conviction that what he does is bad, is an expression of his will. When he agrees to cheat, for instance, the thoughts and beliefs that are normally active in his life momentarily lose their reality for him. He 'forgets' at the time that he abhors what he is tempted to do, or he remembers it only as in a dream or swoon. In this he is like the man who loses his head and runs away or slaps someone in a fit of temper. Freud characterizes the desire and the action which fulfils it as 'ego alien'. We can describe what we have here as a loss of autonomy.

The more difficult cases, although they are continuous with these, are those in which the agent has not achieved autonomy. In the extreme case where he generally acts on impulse we could say that he has no will of his own. He is blown about like a leaf in the wind. But there is a different case where his will is determined 'from inside'. When he acts in accordance with it there is nothing that he acts contrary to, yet his will is not his own. In Freud's terminology here 'the ego is not master in its own house'. If we say of such a man that he is not true to himself, then we must remember that the self to which he is untrue is the self he has not yet found. It is not hidden; it does not yet exist. To find it, as we have seen, is for him to make something of himself. To do so he has to turn in a different direction, and he is prevented from doing so by anxieties and by the defensive postures by means of which he hopes to contain them, and also by positive pursuits to which he has remained anchored since his childhood. Here he is held back not so much from doing as from finding what he wants, from developing into an autonomous person.

One kind of case familiar to psycho-analysis is one in which a person is ruled by an over-strict super-ego — someone, for instance, who is obsessed with doing the right thing, one whom every situation presents with a duty to fulfill. I mention this case because I want to guard against the idea that the direction in which such a person's freedom lies is set by his desires and appetites, so that the freer he becomes the more selfish he is bound to be. This is a misunderstanding on which Freud comments in his *Introductory Lectures*. He says that such a conflict between a repressive moral attitude and repressed desires 'is not resolved by helping one side to win a victory over the other. It is true we see that in neurotics asceticism has gained the day; the result of which is that the suppressed sexual impulses have found a vent for themselves in the symptoms. If we were to make victory possible to the sensual side instead, the disregarded forces repressing sexuality would have to indemnify themselves by symptoms. Neither of these measures will succeed in ending the inner conflict; one side in either event will remain unsatisfied' (1949a, p. 361). Freud makes it quite clear that to advocate either 'free living' or an adherence to 'conventional morality' is to take a facile view of the problems of such a person.

If his moral beliefs drive him on like a slave, if they stop him being himself, the fault does not lie in the values in which he believes, but in his relation to them, in the use he makes of them. What such a man is unable to do is not merely to find pleasure in life, but also to give pleasure to others, kindness and consideration, and so to live more decently. In some cases freedom for such a person may mean extricating himself from being an instrument to evil. I am thinking of the man who oppresses others in the name of fighting the evil in them — he may be a headmaster, a police officer, an inquisitor.

There are many different cases here, but an instance of one such case may be found in Mrs Solness in Ibsen's play *The Master Builder*. In his inaugural lecture on 'Moral Integrity' Professor Winch characterized her plight in the following words:

> She is someone who is obsessed with the Kantian idea of 'acting for the sake of duty'. She does not appear, though, as a paragon of moral purity, but rather as a paradigm of a certain sort of moral corruption. No doubt her constant appeal to duty is a defence against the dangerous and evil resentments she harbours within herself. For all that, it is possible to think that the situation would have been a good deal less evil if she had occasionally forgotten her 'duty' and let herself go. At least this might have cleared the

air and opened the way for some genuine human relationships
between herself and her fellow-characters — relationships which
are conspicuously lacking in the scene as Ibsen presents it. (1968,
pp. 12—13)

Winch says of Mrs Solness that 'her constant appeal to duty is
a *defence* against the dangerous and evil resentments she
harbours within herself'. It is also a defence against the more
sensual aspect of her nature which has not had much chance
to develop under the tight reign in which she has kept it. Her
lack of warmth is partly the result of this and partly an
expression of the chip she carries on her shoulder. For her to
'forget her duty' means to face 'the resentments she harbours
within herself'. It also means facing her own emotional
immaturity and dependence which she fears would leave her
vulnerable to exploitation.

In his paper 'Love and Morality' Ernest Jones speaks of
such defensive morality as 'substitutive morality'. It takes the
place of an 'attitude of love'. Jones is not clear that the latter
is a *moral* attitude and that its relation to 'substitutive morality' is that of what is genuine to what is counterfeit. In taking
the place of an 'attitude of love' it checks warmth, generosity
and compassion. This 'substitution' takes place in the development of a person because the openness demanded by love
represents a danger to him, and because in his particular case
love is inextricably mixed with greed, jealousy and hate. It is
thus a defensive measure and becomes a part of the person's
character, a feature of his whole attitude to life — it 'gives a
characteristic colouring to the whole personality'.

Jones writes: 'With many people this substitution of morality for love proves a fairly successful working basis for life.
They become reliable and decent citizens who play their part
in life well enough. They always suffer, it is true, from the
drawback of never greatly enjoying life, and for their neighbours they present the drawback of being more or less hard-
hearted and intolerant people' (1937, p. 3). He then mentions
extreme cases where the defence in question is not successful
and the failure leads to neurosis or psychosis. Broadly speaking, he mentions two kinds of case: one in which a person
has an exaggerated sense of evil in others, feels persecuted by

this evil and tries to stamp it out with brutality (paranoia), and the other where he has an exaggerated sense of his own evil (melancholia). In both cases one can, in Freud's words, speak of 'the return of the repressed'. What is repressed is the evil in the person which in the first case he sees reflected in others and in the second case feels in his own breast.[1]

To return to the non-extreme case. Jones says that when such a person does what he believes to be his duty, when he does things for other people, when he displays concern for them, though it cannot be said that he acts against his will, nevertheless he doesn't act spontaneously and he is not fully behind his actions. His expressions of concern have a certain urgency; his actions do not come from genuine concern. As he puts it: he does the things he does 'because he feels he ought to'. Jones implies that he does not do them because he really wants to. He contrasts this with those cases where we say, 'He does it out of kindness, love, or thought for others.' The idea is that the obligation he feels compels him to act in a way that love or pity does not. As he puts it: 'This feeling of "oughtness", though in itself often concealed or even repressed, definitely differentiates the attitudes and behaviour from those more spontaneously arising from friendliness, affection and love' (1937, p. 1). When he says that this feeling of 'oughtness' is concealed, he means that the person is deceived in thinking that he does what he wants.

He suggests that while normally there is no question of why a person acts out of kindness, this question is in order in these special cases. Normally a man does not have an ulterior motive for doing what he believes he ought to do. But it is otherwise where the belief serves a defensive purpose. Jones gives an analysis of why in these special cases a man feels he ought to do the kind thing. His analysis has many parts and derives largely from Melanie Klein's work. Briefly it boils down to this. Why does he feel he ought to do the kind thing? Why does he feel he must fulfil his obligations? Because he feels that if he does not he will be swamped by feelings of hatred and resentment, and he will lose his sense of living

[1] In 'Mourning and Melancholia' Freud characterizes this feeling as a species of perception, and not a delusion (see 1950, vol. iv, p. 156).

among people who care for him and for each other, and among whom concern and order are the rule of the day — in short, plunged into a hostile and unpredictable world. His sense of obligation is thus a self-protective measure — a measure for protecting him from retaliation for his own hatred and greed, and also from a sense of worthlessness. It is also a measure for protecting others from his own greed and destructiveness, as well as a means of making up to them for his selfishness.

Discussing Wittgenstein's distinction between an absolute and a relative sense of 'ought', Rush Rhees gave the following example: ' "You ought to make sure that the strip is firmly clasped before you start drilling." "What if I don't?" "When I tell you what will happen if you don't, you see what I mean" ' (1970, p. 96). Jones, similarly, tells us what the kind of people he writes about fear will happen if they disregard what they feel they ought to do. The inner voice which constantly points out their duties is thus an expression of their concern for protection. So the development of what Jones calls a 'moral' attitude in such people as represented by Mrs Solness is an expression of their will or determination to live safely, to keep at bay what is destructive in them.

But what does it hamper? What would such a person be free to do if he did not have to protect himself, defend his image of others, in this way? We should not imagine that if he could be brought to dispense with these defensive measures alternative attitudes and courses of action would immediately become available to him, courses of action which he would then be free to take. No, he would fall a prey to a different tyranny — the tyranny of his emotions. But it is only by facing them — hatred of those he loves, envy of those he admires, greed for what those he needs most possess — that he may, if he is lucky, find a freedom which is at present unthinkable to him. For enduring these emotions, shouldering the responsibility of their burden, may lead to an inner transformation, a reorientation which makes possible new ways of acting, new relationships, and a new toleration of other people's defects and misfortunes. Of Mrs Solness, Winch said: 'If she had occasionally forgotten her "duty" and let herself go, this might have cleared the air and opened the way for some genuine human relationships.' In these words is condensed what may well be a long story of inner struggle that may lead to an inner transformation.

Without such a transformation the removal of a constraining 'moral' attitude would simply lead to a different form of slavery. The ability for more genuine relationships is thus not something that Mrs Solness can be given with the touch of a magic wand — by taking away her obsessions, compulsions or inhibitions. It takes courage, patience and endurance for it to grow, and also the unlearning of habits and the relearning of ways of establishing contact with people. If it were merely a question of being able to let herself go she would only find, as she feared, that she was grabbing, callous and cruel. If she could endure it, though, without protecting herself, without necessarily acting it out in her life, feeling the horror of it all, she might also find genuine love and concern in her heart, see that after all she cares for people, that they matter to her, and that this is why her greed, hatred and resentment are so particularly horrifying. Otherwise she would not have needed to go to such lengths to defend herself and protect others. As what is constructive in her becomes accessible and more directly active in her life, she will be able to make amends, to forgive herself and others, and the pressure from what is grabbing and hating in her will diminish, thus no longer constituting as great a threat to her. It is in this sense that 'forgetting her "duty"' and 'letting herself go' could set her free to look for and grow into more genuine human relationships. When this is achieved she would be freer than she was before, for she would neither have to protect herself nor live in the constant danger of becoming a slave to her passions. This is how the direction in which a man's freedom lies can often only emerge upon the resolution of inner conflict.

This is one kind of case where a person's whole character and orientation to life has become his prison. The simple model of a desire and some constraint preventing its fulfilment, or of a compulsion deflecting someone from keeping a promise or remaining true to his moral beliefs will not fit it. For what we have here is not a person who is forced to act against his will, nor one whose will has become subservient to some alien purpose, but rather someone who is divided against himself — though he does not appreciate this. Whichever way he turns such a person is unfree. Yet his case is also unlike that of a person who is divided in himself — divided between two desires neither of which has a greater claim on him, or divided in his loyalties. That is why I have described him as divided *against* himself. What he needs to find if he is to be free is a new will, and this is not something that he is going to find ready-made. It is something that has to grow and can only do so if he can stop sheltering and deceiving himself. Finding such a will is coming to self-knowledge in the sense explained in chapter 8.

To sum up, then, when Freud spoke of man's lack of freedom and the way its scope can be enlarged, he was thinking primarily of man's mastery over himself so that his actions come from him. The fact that they come from his unconscious by no means guarantees that they come from him. There are many antitheses to such autonomy or self-determination: taking one's lead, one's thoughts and tastes from others, a defensive identification with others, a dependent mode of existence, self-absorption and narcissism, a defensive or compensatory orientation to life, an impaired sense of responsibility. Here a person's will is not his own in the sense that *he* does not determine it. But even though it may not be subject to restrictions or compulsions that are external to it, it cannot be described as free. To find greater freedom such a person would have to achieve greater autonomy. But he cannot do so while remaining untrue to himself, while seeking refuge in evasion and inauthenticity. Freud's characterization of psychoanalysis as an insight-therapy, his assertion that it does no more and no less than enlarge the patient's knowledge of himself, is bound up with this connection between autonomy and authenticity. But this is the subject of another book, *Insight and Therapy*, which I hope to write.

Bibliography

Anderson, John, 1940. 'Freudianism and Society', *Australasian Journal of Psychology and Philosophy*

Alston, William, P., 1977. 'Self-Intervention and the Structure of Motivation', in *The Self: Psychological and Philosophical Issues*, ed. Theodore Mischel (Blackwell)

Austin, J. L., 1961. 'A Plea for Excuses', *Philosophical Papers*, ed. J. O. Urmson and G. J. Warnock (Clarendon Press)

Brill, A. A., 1948. *Lectures on Psycho-Analytic Psychiatry* (John Lehmann)

Descartes, René, 1954. *Philosophical Writings*, trans. and ed. G. E. M. Anscombe and P. Geach (Nelson)

Dilman, İlham, 1966. 'Professor Malcolm on Dreams', *Analysis*

—— 1972. 'Is the Unconscious a Theoretical Construct?', *The Monist*

—— 1973a. *Induction and Deduction: A Study in Wittgenstein* (Blackwell)

—— 1973b. 'Freud and Psychological Determinism', *The Human World*

—— 1974. 'Philosophy and Psychiatry', *The Human World*

—— 1975. *Matter and Mind: Two Essays in Epistemology* (Macmillan)

—— 1976. 'Socrates and Dostoyevsky on Punishment', *Philosophy and Literature*

—— 1979. *Morality and the Inner Life: A Study in Plato's Gorgias* (Macmillan)

—— 1981. *Studies in Language and Reason* (Macmillan)

—— 1983. *Freud and Human Nature* (Blackwell)

—— 1984. 'Our Knowledge of Other People', in *Philosophy and Life: Essays for Wisdom*, ed. İlham Dilman (Martinus Nijhoff)

—— and Phillips, D. Z., 1971. *Sense and Delusion* (Routledge)

Dostoyevsky, Fyodor, 1950. *The Eternal Husband*, trans. Constance Garnett (Heinemann)

—— 1955. *The Idiot*, trans. David Magarshack (Penguin)

—— 1956. *Crime and Punishment*, trans. David Magarshack (Penguin)

Drury, M. O'C., 1974. 'Fact and Hypothesis', *The Human World*

Field, G. C. 1922. 'Is the Conception of the Unconscious of Value in Psychology?', *Mind*

Frankl, Viktor, E., 1967. *Man's Search for Meaning* (Washington Square Press)

Freud, Sigmund 1933. *New Introductory Lectures on Psycho-Analysis*, trans. W. J. H. Sprott (W. W. Norton)

—— 1947. *The Question of Lay Analysis*, trans. Nancy Procter-Gregg (Imago)

—— 1948a. *Beyond the Pleasure Principle*, trans. C. J. M. Hubback (Hogarth Press)

—— 1948b. *An Autobiographical Study*, trans. James Strachey (Hogarth Press)

—— 1949a. *Introductory Lectures on Psycho-Analysis*, trans. Joan Riviére (Allen and Unwin)

—— 1949b. *The Ego and the Id*, trans. James Strachey (Hogarth Press)

—— 1949c. *An Outline of Psycho-Analysis*, trans. James Strachey (Hogarth Press)

—— 1949d. *Civilization and its Discontents*, trans. James Strachey (Hogarth Press)

—— 1950. *Collected Papers*, vols. i—v, trans. Joan Riviére (Hogarth Press)

—— 1954a. *The Origins of Psycho-Analysis: Letters to Wilhelm Fliess, Drafts and Notes, 1887—1902*, ed. M. Bonaparte, Anna Freud and Ernst Kriss, trans. E. Mosbacker and James Strachey (Imago)

—— 1954b. *Psychopathology of Everyday Life*, trans. A. A. Brill (Ernest Benn)

—— 1957. *Complete Psychological Works*, trans. James Strachey (Hogarth Press)

—— 1967. *The Interpretation of Dreams*, trans. James Strachey (Avon Books)

—— and Breuer, Joseph, 1950. *Studies in Hysteria*, trans. A. A. Brill (Beacon Press)

Fromm, Erich, 1950. *Man for Himself* (Routledge and Kegan Paul)

Gide, André, 1922. *Les Caves du Vatican* (Gallimard)

Groddeck, Georg, 1950. *The Book of the It*, trans. V. M. E. Collins (Vision Press)

Guntrip, Harry, 1964. *Healing the Sick Mind* (Unwin Books)

—— 1977. *Personality Structure and Human Interaction* (Hogarth Press)

Hamlyn, D. W., 1977. 'Self-Knowledge', in *The Self: Psychological and Philosophical Issues*, ed. Theodore Mischel (Blackwell)

Hampshire, Stuart, 1959. *Thought and Action* (Chatto and Windus)

—— 1961. 'Feeling and Expression', Inaugural Lecture (H. K. Lewis)

—— 1974. 'Disposition and Memory', in *Freud: A Collection of Critical Essays*, ed. Richard Wollheim (Anchor Books)

Hoggart, Richard, 1971. 'Only Connect — Reith Lecture 1', *The Listener*, 18 Nov.

Hume, David, 1957. *An Inquiry Concerning the Principles of Morals* (Library of Liberal Arts)

Ibsen, Henrik, 1971. 'The Master Builder', in *The Master Builder and Other Plays* (Penguin)

Isaacs, Susan, 1952. 'The Nature and Function of Phantasy', in *Developments in Psycho-Analysis*, ed. Joan Rivière (Hogarth Press)

Jones, Ernest, 1937. 'Love and Morality', *International Journal of Psycho-Analysis*, Jan.

—— 1954, 1957. *Sigmund Freud: Life and Work*, vols i and iii (Hogarth Press)

—— 1974. 'Free Will and Determinism', in *Psycho-Myth, Psycho-History*, vol. ii (Hillstone)

Jung, C. G., 1940. *The Integration of the Personality*, trans. Stanley M. Dell (Kegan Paul, Trench, Trubner)

Kafka, Franz, 1948. *The Diaries*, vol. i (1910—13), ed. Max Brod (Secker and Warburg)

Kant, Immanuel, 1959. *Fundamental Principles of the Metaphysic of Ethics*, trans. T. K. Abbott (Longmans)

Klein, Melanie, 1948. 'The Early Development of Conscience in the Child', in *Psycho-Analysis To-day*, ed. Sándor Lorand (Allen and Unwin)

—— 1952. 'Some Theoretical Conclusions Regarding the Emotional Life of the Infant', in *Developments in Psycho-Analysis*, ed. Joan Rivière (Hogarth Press)

—— 1960. 'Our Adult World and its Roots in Infancy' (Tavistock pamphlet)

Laird, John, 1922. 'Is the Conception of the Unconscious of Value in Psychology?', *Mind*

Locke, John, 1959. *An Essay Concerning Human Understanding* (Everyman)

Mach, Ernst, 1898. 'On the Principle of Comparison in Physics', *Popular Scientific Lectures*, trans. Thomas J. McCormack (Open Court, Chicago)

Macmurray, John, 1933. *Freedom in the Modern World* (Faber and Faber)

Malcolm, Norman, 1967. *Ludwig Wittgenstein: A Memoir* (Oxford University Press)

—— 1977. 'Behaviourism as a Philosophy of Psychology', in *Thought and Knowledge* (Cornell University Press)

Malinowski, Bronislaw, 1955. *Sex and Repression in Savage Society* (Meridian Books)
Money-Kryle, R. E., 1955. 'Psycho-Analysis and Ethics', in *New Directions in Psycho-Analysis*, ed. Melanie Klein, Paula Heimann and Roger Money-Kyrle (Tavistock)
Moore, G. E., 1947. 'Free Will', *Ethics* (Oxford University Press)
Murdock, Iris, 1953. *Sartre* (Bowes and Bowes)
Nietzsche, Friedrich, 1972. *Twilight of the Idols and the Anti-Christ* (Penguin)
Overstreet, Harry and Overstreet, Bonaro, 1954. *The Mind Alive* (W. W. Norton)
Plato, 1955. 'Phaedo', in *The Last Days of Sacrates* (Penguin)
—— 1973a. *Gorgias* (Penguin)
—— 1973b. 'Phaedrus', in *Phaedrus and Letters VII and VIII* (Penguin)
Proust, Marcel, 1952. *In Remembrance of Things Past*, trans. C. K. Scott Moncrieff (Chatto and Windus)
—— 1954. *A La Recherche du Temps Perdu*, vols i—iii (N. R. F., Bibliothèque de la Pléiade)
Puner, Helen Walker, 1959. *Freud: His Life and His Mind* (Dell Publishing Co.)
Rhees, Rush, 1970. 'Wittgenstein's Builders' and 'Some Developments in Wittgenstein's View of Ethics', in *Discussions of Wittgenstein* (Routledge and Kegan Paul)
Robinson, Ian, 1975. 'Notes on the Language of Love I', in *The Survival of English* (Cambridge University Press)
Sartre, Jean-Paul, 1943. *L'Être et le Néant* (Gallimard)
—— 1947. 'Une idée fondamentale de la phénoménologie de Husserl: L'Intentionnalité', in *Situations I* (Gallimard)
—— 1948. *Esquisse d'une Théorie des Emotions* (Hermann)
—— 1949. 'La République du Silence', in *Situations III* (Gallimard)
—— 1970. *Existentialism and Humanism*, trans. Philip Mairet (Methuen)
Schopenhauer, Arthur, 1951. 'Free Will and Fatalism' and 'Character', in *Essays: On Human Nature* (Allen and Unwin)
Segal, Hanna, 1964. *Introduction to the Work of Melanie Klein* (Heinemann)
Shakespeare, William, 1947. 'Othello, the Moor of Venice', *The Complete Works* (Oxford University Press)
Snodgrass, W. D., 1960. 'Crime for Punishment: The Tenor of Part One', *The Hudson Review*, Spring
Taylor, Charles, 1977. 'What is Human Agency?', in *The Self: Psychological and Philosophical Issues*, ed. Theodore Mischel (Blackwell)
Tolstoy, Leo, 1956. *Anna Karenina*, trans. Rosemary Edmonds (Penguin)
—— 1960. 'The Kreutzer Sonata' and 'Father Sergius', in *The Kreutzer*

Sonata and Other Tales, trans. Aylmer Maude (Oxford University Press)

Winch, Peter, 1968. 'Moral Integrity' Inaugural Lecture (Blackwell). Reprinted 1972 *Ethics and Action* (Routledge)

Wisdom, John, 1952. *Other Minds* (Blackwell)

—— 1953. *Philosophy and Psycho-Analysis* (Blackwell)

—— 1965. *Paradox and Discovery* (Blackwell)

Wittgenstein, Ludwig, 1961. *Tractatus Logico-Philosophicus*, trans. David Pears and B. M. McGuinness (Routledge)

—— 1963. *Philosophical Investigations* (Blackwell)

—— 1966. 'Conversations on Freud', in *Lectures and Conversations on Aesthetics, Psychology and Religious Belief*, ed. Cyril Barrett (Blackwell)

—— 1967. *Zettel* (Blackwell)

—— 1969a. *The Blue and Brown Books* (Blackwell)

—— 1969b. *On Certainty* (Blackwell)

Wortis, Joseph, 1954. *Fragments of an Analysis with Freud* (Simon and Schuster)

Index